(To: Pam
Remember ... t
each day, # 331
Joan)

Published by
Designs 4 Crochet LLc
P O Box 6904
West Palm Beach, FL 33405
Email: a0crochetjad@msn.com

ISBN: 0-615-27223-1
978-0-615-27223-8

Mission Statement
Teaching the love of crochet to one person at a time.

336 Crochet Tips !
The Solutions Book for Crocheters

All Rights Reserved

Copyrights

336
Crochet Tips !

The Solutions book
for Crocheters

Joan A. Davis
Certified Crochet Instructor
Member of the Crochet Guild of America

"There is a magic in getting just what you want, the way you want it. And there is a magic in the feeling of pride and accomplishment in doing something for yourself, and doing it well..."
Maggie Righetti,
Sweater Design in Plain English
(My mentor when we lived in Atlanta, GA)

Table of Contents

336 Crochet Tips !
The Solutions Book for Crocheters

Dedication

336 Crochet Tips! is dedicated to the following Ancestral Mothers who helped me learn to crochet at a youthful time when crochet was not on my mind:

The Late Leila Eason Collins, My Great-grandmother
The Late Ossie Collins Rogers, My Maternal Grandmother
The Late Ruth Rogers Davis, My Mother
The Late Zelma Johnson, My Paternal Grandmother

To My Sisters:
Audrey Davis-Jones and Oreida Davis-Hanson
To My Brothers:
Anthony B. Davis, Roger W. Davis, Derek A. Davis, Jeffrey E. Davis, and Maurice M. Davis
To My Son, Arnold Nigel Gantz
To My Grandchildren: Arnold, DJ, Nicholas, Aniya, Joshua

To my friends Carol Bartlebaugh,
Joyce Renee Wyatt, and Myra Wood
To my crochet students and crochet professionals who have worked with me through the years; to the School District of Palm Beach County Community School Division for helping me get the crochet program introduced to the public.

To all of you, please accept my gratitude, and I thank you for being in my life to help me along the Journey.

Preface

336 Crochet Tips! Originated as a result of my students asking many questions during my classes, and from the many calls for help.   I kept a log book of all the answers to the students questions, so that I did not have research each time the same questions arose.   The collection of answers kept growing.   Out of curiosity one day, I began to count the tips.

336 Crochet Tips! has many of the tips and bits of information you need in one place. You would have to look in many different books, references or resources--some resources you may have and some you may not. The hand-book is designed so that you can carry in your crochet kit.

Select a topic you would like to explore.   Read through the chapter.   You can pick and choose topics at random; and do not have to feel obligated to read the book sequentially.   You may want to concentrate on certain tips, while other tips may be more relevant at some other time in your crochet project explorations. Some tips are repeated because they are apropos to different topics.

Enjoy **336 Crochet Tips!** The Solutions Book For Crocheters
With Universal Love,
Joan A. Davis
Riviera Beach, Florida
January, 2009

336 Crochet Tips !
The Solutions Book for Crocheters

336 Crochet Tips !
The Solutions Book for Crocheters

TIP # 1
UNDERSTANDING QUALITY AND EXCELLENCE

Crochet is known to bring comfort into our lives. Sometimes it helps us reduce stress; it brings joy to our heart to see the yarn forms wonderful items we love to share.

Quality is a skill acquired mainly through touch and experience. Quality work is crucial. Crochet fashions of high quality materials but poorly constructed, poorly finished and poorly fitted are a total waste of time and effort.

Create many opportunities to crochet to improve your skill. Quality material and quality workmanship produce a pleasure and a satisfaction for the crocheter that is as soul soothing as meditation, or a cool drink on a hot summer's day.

Sometimes the yarns can be remodeled; some yarns can be pulled out (except perhaps mohair and novelty yarns) and re-crocheted. Cost is not a reliable criteria although quality is not "cheap".

TIPS # 2 - 8

⌘ Learn to Read the Yarn Label .

⌘ Learn the FEEL of the yarn.

⌘ Take time to match hook size to yarn

⌘ Make a good size practice swatch of about 4" x 4"

⌘ Stitches should not be too loose nor too tight.

⌘ Try to use quality yarns and threads. They last a long time and can stand up to wear.

⌘ Once crochet basics have been mastered through touch and experience, this contributes to QUALITY OF LIFE! And quality of life reduces stress.

336 Crochet Tips !
The Solutions Book for Crocheters

336 Crochet Tips !
The Solutions Book for Crocheters

My Own
Crochet Tips !

Chapter 2

TIPS #9 - 15

⌘ Quell the excitement of the "yarn".

⌘ Think wisely about your crochet investment.

⌘ Read Your pattern, first.

⌘ Make a practice swatch to get used to the yarn and the hook and the stitch pattern. This is called making a gauge swatch. In that way if you "goof" up, you have not goofed up on your project.

⌘ Change hooks, if necessary, to achieve the recommended number of stitches and rows listed in the pattern.

⌘ Keep your crochet kit with adequate supplies, so that you are not "running" out of basics kit item. [1]

PLAN AHEAD!

Before you begin a new row, unwind enough yarn to complete the new row, or next cluster if you are working motifs. Make this a habit to keep your tension constant. The tug of short yarn will change your tension and make the crochet uneven.

The second reason is that you will find out *before* you run out of yarn that you don't have enough to finish the row. It is false economy to use half a row of yarn and to have an unnecessary join in the middle of a row, and you will have two ends to hide in the middle of the row. Make the join at the end of the preceding row. Cut the extra yarn off and use it for seams, markers, surface embroidery, or stash it away for granny squares.

---

[1] **Donna Kooler's Encyclopedia of Crochet, Copyrighted 2002**

Tip #16

Take your own notes. Sometimes, no matter how clear a crochet designer thinks the instructions are written, the instructions are still not "clear" enough for you.   Take your own notes, so you will understand.   Use a "Post-It" type of portable note to stick on the pattern.

1.

2.

3.

4.

5.

6.

7.

8.

9.

10.

11.

12.

13.

14.

15.

16.

17.

18.

19.

20.

21.

22.

23.

24.

25.

26.

27.

28.

29.

30.

What Goes Into The Basic Crochet Kit

Chapter 3

TIP # 17

The **Basic Crochet kit** contains everything you need at your disposal to crochet any project—including a durable tote to carry the kit and yarns.

TIP # 18

▶▶ Recommendation! ◀◀

Add to your crochet kit little by little until you have all the items on the list. At some point in time you will need an item and your favorite crafts store may be closed in the middle of night—just when you needed an important item.

TIP # 19
KEEP YOUR KIT ORGANIZED

TIP # 20
Do not use dark colors to learn a new technique.

TIP #21
For practice, use   plain yarns not fuzzy nor fancy nor novelty yarns.

TIP # 22

Here is what the basic crochet kit contains:

- A good Reference Book for crochet basics, such as *336 CROCHET TIPS ! The Solutions Book For Crocheters.*
- Crochet Hooks in various sizes: Preferably aluminum hooks sizes: B (2.25mm) to K (6.50mm)
- Crochet Hooks Container
- Yarn (for practice) worsted weight in light or bright colors [1]. Yarns can be 100 percent wool or wool blend, or acrylic.
- Scissors; or other cutting implement.   [2]Dental floss in your kit is excellent for traveling.   All you need to use is the cutter, then you don't have use scissors.
- Reading Glasses, if needed,
- Pens or pencils; and Highlighter (your choice of color
- Notebook or paper for notes, highlighter, any color of your preference
- Paper clips (About 4 or 5)
- "Post It" or other self sticking notes, preferably .3 x 5 ; or 4 x size.
- Small brass safety pins; or other types of markers for counting stitches and marking location on the crochet.
- Big Eye Steel Yarn needle
- Yarn Bobbins
- Gauge measurer, or clear ruler or quilter's square ruler, or tape measure.
- Bag or tote that is unique to you to keep crochet materials organized.

---

[1] Do not use dark colors to learn a new technique. For practice, use   plain non-fuzzy nor fancy yarns..

[2] The cutter can be used instead of scissors, and the dental floss won't be confiscated on airplanes like scissors can be.

Beyond the Basics for the Advanced Beginner and beyond—A few additional materials for the crochet kit.

TIP #23

These Items are for the advance Crocheter:

• Steel Hooks (See Hooks Chart) • Crochet Thread in size #10 or 20 • Afghan/Tunisian hooks in various sizes	• Double-ended crochet hooks • Hairpin Loom • Graph paper (4-; or 5-; 6-; or 8- square to the inch/cm

TIPS # 24 - 26

If you are taking a crochet class, these are the recommendations:

Bring lots of patience, courage and enthusiasm.
Sometimes adults forget that there is a learning curve, just like there is for children. Be patient with yourself while learning. Practice crochet techniques at least ten minutes per day

Ask questions
Bring lots of questions for the instructor. This is your time to get answers. Asking questions always facilitates positive learning. Qualified instructors can handle the questions. Have an enquiring mind.

Don't rip & pull out your crochet so many times.
Bring the crochet problem pieces to class. The instructor can only help you if you have the courage to bring problem cases & projects to class. An instructor can offer simple solutions if she/he can "See" the problem.

336 Crochet Tips !
The Solutions Book for Crocheters

Crochet Basics
Chapter 4

Crochet Basics   Chapter 4

**There are many books written on the crochet basics. This
section is intended for refresher and reference only.**

TIP # 27

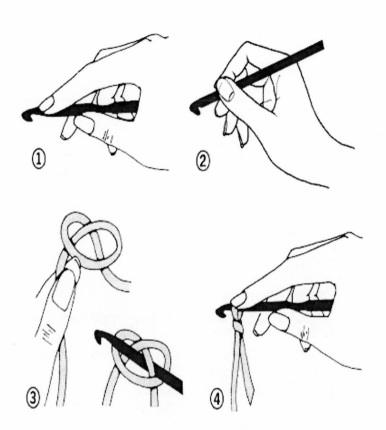

Getting Started

There are 2 ways to hold the hook:
- ⌘ **(1) as though you are holding a steak knife or**
- ⌘ **(2) as though, you are holding a pencil.**
- ⌘ **Make a slip knot to hold the working loop.   NOTE: The working loop is not counted as a stitch.**

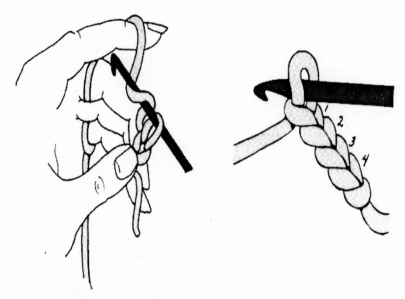

⌘ Thread your tension hand, **which is the opposite hand you crochet with.**

⌘ With the working loop on your hook, yarn over and pull through the loop on the hook. This is called "foundation chain stitch". Some patterns will count this as "Row 1", and some patterns will refer to simply as "foundation row". Begin the actual pattern stitch after crocheting in the foundation row.

⌘ Count stitches from the stitch which is closest to the hook. Do not count the working loop on the hook as a stitch.

⌘ After the chain st is worked turn it over to the back side of the stitch, so that you can see the bump side of the chain.

⌘ You can work the foundation chain from the front side of the chain. Or, you can work from the bump side of the chain.

⌘ When you work stitches into the bump side of the chain—which is the "back" of the chain, it makes a much smoother finish when you add an edging.

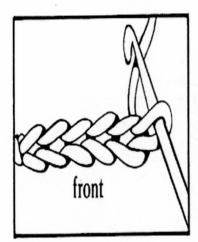

front

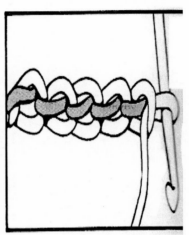

TIP # 28

Here is How to Pick up the Foundation Row of Stitches After you have made the Chain:

Method 1   Method 2

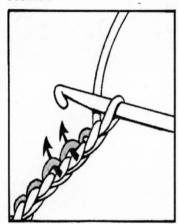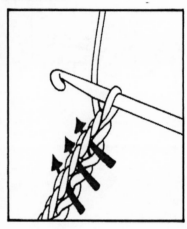

TIP 29

There are two ways to enter the chain when starting the first row: (1) under the bump on the back of the chain.   By entering the chain (ch) under the bump, you will have a smoother finish.   **Method 1 is recommended.**

(2) Or, you can enter the foundation chain through the middle of the chain stitch .

TIP # 30

When you enter the foundation stitch through the front of the stitch, this weakens the bottom of the ch st when you have to add an edging or finishing.

TIP # 31

Chain st is the foundation of all crochet stitches; and must be worked for each new project.   Each stitch creates its own chain stitch on the top of the previous stitch just worked.

TIP #32

If you can *read* international crochet patterns, then when you travel to far-away places, then you can pick up a crochet book from any country and follow the pattern. While you may not know what thread or hook size, because of the language barrier, you will be able to follow the actual crochet pattern.   A good photo will indicate if you are to work with thread or yarn.   International crochet style is based upon mainly symbols, which does not change from country to country.   The symbols remain the same.

TIP #33

There are more than 66 of these crochet symbols.   Once you understand them, experiment *reading* the symbols, you can crochet your patterns a lot faster than reading, interpreting, and trying to crochet the standard American word pattern.   Some crocheters appreciate knowing both methods: The American Word patterns along side of the "international" crochet symbol patterns;   therefore, many American publishers, writers, and designers are moving toward including both methods of pattern interpretation.

TIP # 34
The Basic Stitches, in American Terminology

	Symbols	Abbreviations and Brief Explanation
1.	∞∞∞∞	**Ch.** All crochet begins with the ch st
2.	XXXX	**Sc.** Single crochet. Shortest **of** the basic sts. Uses chain 1 to turn on the end of the row.
3.	TTTT	**Hdc**. Half Double Crochet. Next in height. First of "yarn over" stitches— means that it begins with a yarn over the hook before you work the stitch. Uses chain 2 to turn on the end of the row.
4.	₮₮₮₮	**Dc.** Double Crochet. Next in height; and is the "workhorse" stitch. It , too, begins, with a Yarn over the hook. Most crochet patterns use this stitch. Uses chain 3 to turn on the end of the row. However, you can use a chain 2 to turn if you have a large crochet hand style. The chain-2 turn will prevent chain stitches from creating "elbows" on the edges of your work, and the items will have straighter edges.
5.	₮₮₮₮	**Tr or trc.** Triple Crochet or Treble crochet. Tallest of the basic stitches. It begins with 2 yarn overs. These yarn overs are worked off in groups of 2 "pull through" at a time. Uses chain 3 to turn at the end of a row.
6.	ⱴ	**Sc inc.** Single crochet increase. Two sc sts are worked into same st.
7.	V	**Hdc inc.** Half Double crochet increase. 2 hdc are worked into same st.

8.	V	*Dc inc*. Double crochet *increase*. 2 dc are worked into same st.
9.	V	*Trc or tr inc*. Triple crochet increase. 2 trc are worked into the same stitch.
10.	⋀	*Sc dec.* Single crochet decrease. 2 sc stitches worked into one stitch. A decrease can be made by simply skipping the next stitch. This leaves a hole. The "invisible" decrease is best. To work the invisible single crochet: with working loop on hook, go into next stitch, YO pull through, see 2 loops on hk and leave them on the hk; go into next st, YO and pull through; see 3 loops on hk, YO and pull thru all 3 loops in one motion. See Chapter 18 in *336 Crochet Tips !*
11.	⋀	*Hdc dec.* Half double crochet decrease: Yarn over (YO), into the next st. YO pull thru. See 3 loops on hk. YO pull thru 2 loops and **go into the next st with 2 loops still on hk;** YO, pull thru all 4 loops on hk.
12.	⋀	*Dc dec.* Double Crochet decrease. YO, into the next st. YO pull thru. See 3 loops on hk. YO pull thru 2 loops and **go into the next st with 2 loops still on hk;** YO, pull thru 2 loops, then YO pull thru all 3 loops on hk.
13.	⋀	*Trc or tr dec*. Triple Crochet Decrease. YO 2 times; into the next st, YO pull thru 2 loops, 2 times. See 2 loops left on hk. YO 2 more times, and go into the next st. YO pull thru 2 loops 2 times; then YO pull thru remaining loops on hk in one motion.

14.	●	Sl st. Slip Stitch. This st does not add height, but simply moves the crochet over to begin at a new location. (sometimes this stitch is confused with the sc). This st has one less YO than a sc.

Crochet Symbols from Knitware, British Columbia, Canada

TIP #35

⌘   End off work by YO and pull thru the loop on the hook, 2 times.

TIP #36
Reminder

When working an international type crochet pattern you "read" the pattern in the direction that you crochet. For example; you crochet from the bottom of the item, upward, then you read the pattern from the bottom, upward:

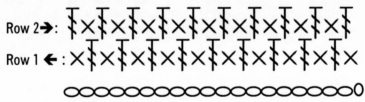

Row 2➔:
Row 1 ⬅ :

The pattern reads: chain 20. If you are a right hand crocheter, on Row 1, read the pattern from the right side to the left on row 1. Working in the back of chains, skip first chain. Sc in 2nd ch from hook, triple crochet in next stitch.   Now, follow the international pattern above.

Stitch notes:

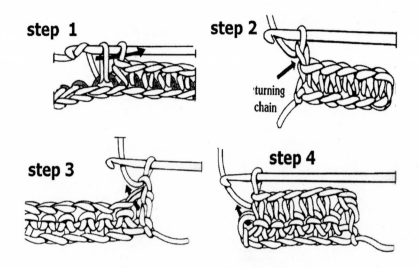

step 1

step 2

'turning
chain

step 3

step 4

TIP # 37
Single Crochet

⌘ **Step 1:** * Enter the chain from the back and under the bump; YO pull the hook thru the bump's loop. See 2 loops on hook. YO pull thru both loops on hook to work the sc. * Repeat from * to next * continue in this method until you reach the end of the row. _REMINDER: The bump is only on the foundation chain row._

⌘ **Step 2:**   Single crochet requires 1 chain st to turn.   This will 1 chain st will equal the height of 1 sc.   _REMINDER: CH 1 & TURN WORK SO THE WORKING LOOP AND HOOK ARE ON YOUR RIGHT IF YOU ARE A RIGHT-HAND CROCHETER.   IF YOU ARE A LEFT-HAND CROCHETER, BEGIN YOUR WORK ON THE LEFT SIDE._

⌘ **Step 3:** When the second row of sc is worked the sequence of steps is just a bit different, because you do not work into a bump. *Insert hook under both parts of the top sc, which looks like the ch; YO and pull thru. _SEE 2 LOOPS ON HOOK._ YO and pull thru both loops to form sc on the second row and all other rows. *   Repeat from * to next * , continue across row.

⌘ **Step 4: Finding the last sc stitch may be a little challenging.**
It is between turning ch on the row below & the last sc on row 1.
Insert hook there. Complete last sc.

      REMINDER: Count stitches for accuracy.

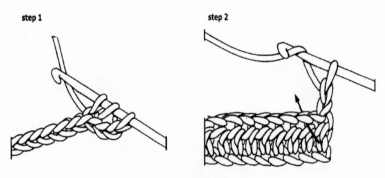

step 1   step 2

TIP #38
Half Double Crochet

1. Work any number of ch sts; plus 2 more. Then Yarn over (YO).
2. Working under the 3rd bump loop on the back of the chain, pull
    through. See 3 loops on hook, as in "Step 1". YO and pull thru
    all 3 loops in one motion.
3.   * YO, work under next bump loop, YO, pull thru bump loop on
    back of ch. See 3 loops on hook, as in "Step 1". YO and pull thru all
    3 loops in one motion *. Repeat from * to next * across row. Ch 2
    to turn.

TIPS # 39 - 42
Half Double Crochet Notes

⌘ Hdc is 1/3 taller than the sc and 1/3 shorter than the double crochet.

⌘ The hdc creates 2 ch stitch patterns: (1) along the top of the stitch, which
is usual for all crochet stitches; and (2) along the back, which appears to
be a chain stitch on its side. This causes a bit of confusion for first time
crocheters.

⌘ On rows 2 and beyond, hook should enter under the chain st on the top hdc and **through the center of the side chain on the back.** *Reminder: Do not work under the side chain st on back of hdc.*

⌘ **To turn your work with hdc, you have to chain 2 to turn. This creates a selvage edge the height of the first hdc to be worked.**

TIP # 43
Double Crochet Stitch

When starting the first row, work the Double Crochet from the bump or back of the Foundation Chain

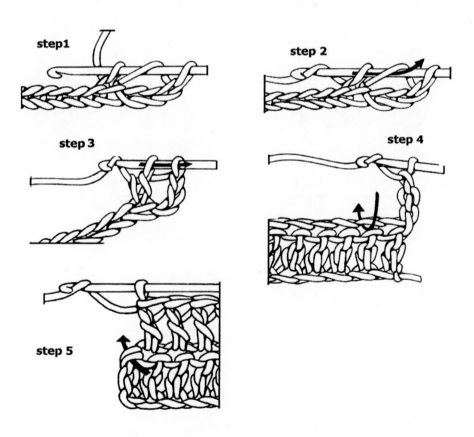

step1

step 2

step 3

step 4

step 5

TIP # 44

If you chain 2 to turn on the double crochet, and do not skip the first dc on the row below, THEN your edges will be straighter.

1. If you are at the end of the row, and ready to begin the next row, chain 2 to turn on the dc, YO Insert hook into first double crochet stitch.
2. YO, pull thru and See 3 loops on hook. YO pull thru 2 loops;
3. YO pull thru 2 loops.
4. Repeat steps 2 and 3 across row.
5. For rows 2 and beyond, using chain 2 to turn, YO then insert hook into first double crochet stitch on the row below so as to create a selvage. * YO, pull thru. [see 3 loops], YO pull thru 2 loops, YO pull thru 2 loops. *. Rep from * to next * across row.
6. Optional Method: In the last dc and the tch, work **dc2tog**: YO, insert hook into the next st, YO, pull through; YO pull through 2 loops. See 2 loops on hook. YO, insert hook in the next st, YO, pull through. See 4 loops on the hook ..YO, pull through 2 loops. YO, pull through 3 loops in one motion. Dc2tog made.
7. Be sure to count your stitches so that you have the recommended number of stitches that are called for in the pattern.

TIPS #45 - 51
Double Crochet Tips:

⌘ Dc is the workhorse stitch of crochet. The dc and the ch st are used more than any other stitches in crocheting.

⌘ Dc is twice as tall as the sc, and 1/3 taller than the hdc.

⌘ Some crocheters will have to use ch 3 to turn, as is required by most patterns; and some crocheters will have to use ch 2 to turn.

⌘ Ch-2 to turn is used when the turning chs create a large bowing effect on the edges of the crochet. In order to straighten this edge, chain 2 is used rather than ch-3.

⌘ If the crocheter uses ch-2 to turn, then the hook is inserted into the 3rd chain from the hook on the foundation row, rather than 4th chain from the hook.

⌘ For rows 2 and beyond regarding the turning chains: Some patterns require that the turning chain be used as a stitch—some patterns require the turning chain to be used as a selvage edge to create a better edge.

⌘ If the tch-2 is used as a selvage edge, the first dc stitch is worked into the very first dc on the prev row. The last 2 sts are worked as a dc2tog.   This creates a selvage on both ends of the row.

TIP # 52
Triple Crochet From the Bump Loop of chain:

1. YO 2 times, Insert hook underneath the bump loop on the back of the ch.
2. YO, pull thru. See 4 loops on the hook. [YO, pull thru] 3 times.

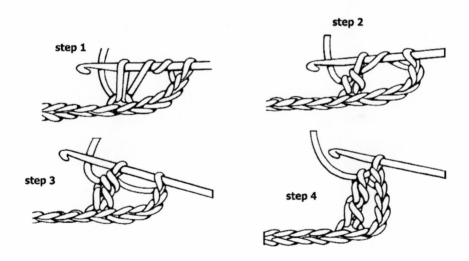

step 1

step 2

step 3

step 4

Tips # 53 & 54

⌘ Because of the height of the trc, a natural space is created between stitches.

⌘ When the trc and sc are worked, alternately, an interesting pattern will develop.

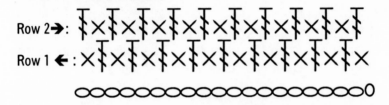

Row 2➜:

Row 1 ⬅ :

TIP #55: LEFT HAND BASICS

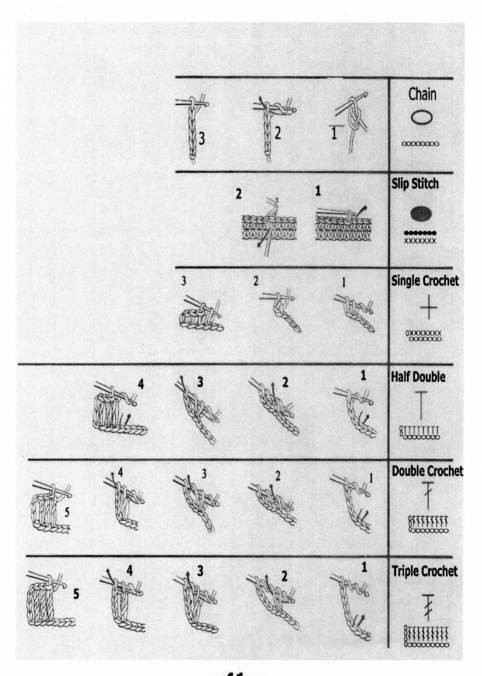

MY CROCHET TIPS !
MY SOLUTIONS

Massage Your Hands

Section 5

336 Crochet Tips !
The Solutions Book for Crocheters

Tip # 56
Massage your hands before
Beginning to crochet

Several years ago, "massage" was reserved for the elite who could afford expensive spas. Now, everyone enjoys the healthful benefits. People who have arthritis or carpal tunnel syndrome well understand, massaging your hands is a very important function, even if you are not working on crafts.

Tip # 57

Use a **light-weight hand cream** with natural colloidal oatmeal, for example Aveeno Hand Lotion. This type of hand cream disappears quickly, and is non-greasy--Unlike some lotions, which are heavy and leave a residue on hands and yarns. Heavy lotions may stain yarns.

Massage the **left hand** by pressing the right-hand thumb into the center of the left-hand palm. Repeat for the right hand.

Move the **thumb in circles** starting with small circles in the center of the palm and move outward. **Vis-à-vis for the right hand.**

Press each pair of fingers and thumbs together as if to pray or clap. Rub hands together quickly to create friction and warmth.

Start at the base of each finger, massage with the opposite hand, all way to the end of each finger and thumb.

Massage your hands again when you finish crocheting.

Use this method to massage your hands whenever you are working on the computer; gardening; writing or any activity in which your hands must stay in the same position for a long period of time.

Take good care of your hands ! Get a manicure every now and then and your hands will appreciate it.

Reading Crochet Patterns With American Abbreviations

Chapter 6

TIP # 58
READING AN AMERICAN CROCHET PATTERN CAN BE MADE EASIER, IF YOU KNOW THE CROCHET ABBREVIATIONS.

In order to write many patterns and save space, writers, crochet designers and publishers write crochet patterns in a code called "Crochet Abbreviations."

Most crocheters do not like to learn "the code". I must admit some of the abbreviations require a lot of thought; however, if you...

TIP # 59

Take the time to memorized the basic crochet abbreviations, you will have a wealth of knowledge of how to read and interpret a crochet pattern. At least, keep these Crochet Tips! near your pattern for reference.

TIP # 60

There are approximately 75 international crochet symbols (depending upon which international reference book used), and approximately 66 of the word abbreviations are used in commercial pattern writing. The Craft Yarn Council of America's Master Crochet abbreviations is included here as well as the frequently used abbreviations.

TIP # 61

▶▶ **NOTE:** Some abbreviations may have double meanings; such as, "RS" which stands for right side (public side of the garment) or right hand side of a garment. Be sure to read all the notes before beginning a pattern, so that you will understand if the designer means right-hand side or public side.◀◀

TIP # 62

The following list has **the basic set of American abbreviations** most frequently used in the crochet industry. When a designer uses an abbreviation not listed here, there is a detailed explanation, usually at the beginning of a pattern; and many designers, writers, and publishers even provide graphics for a clearer explanation.

	Crochet Abbreviations Basic List (In Alpha order after the symbols)	
	Abbreviations	**Descriptions**
1.	**[ ]** **Brackets**	Work instruction with brackets as many times as directed
2.	**( )** **Parentheses**	Used for information and clarity; also work instructions within ( ) as many times as directed
3.	✳ **Asterisk**	Repeat the instructions following the single ✳ as instructed
4.	✳ ... ✳ **Paired Asterisks**	Repeat the instructions between ✳ ... ✳ as many times as directed or repeat from a given set of instructions
5.	**"**	Inch or inches
6.	**Alt**	Alternate
7.	**Approx**	Approximately
8.	**Beg**	Begin/beginning
9.	**Bet**	Between
10.	**BL**	Back loop(s)
11.	**bo**	Bobble
12.	**BP**	Back post
13.	**BPdc**	Back post double crochet
14.	**BPsc**	Back post single crochet
15.	**BPtr**	Back post triple crochet
16.	**CA**	Color A
17.	**CB**	Color B
18.	**CC**	Contrasting color

Crochet Abbreviations Basic List
(In Alpha order after the symbols)

	Abbreviations	Descriptions
19.	Ch	Chain stitch
20.	Ch-	Refers to chain or space previously made. For example: ch-1Space
21.	Ch-sp	Chain space
22.	Cl	Cluster
23.	Cm	Centimeter(s) . 1 cm = .394 inches
24.	Contin	Continue
25.	Dc	Double crochet
26.	Dc2tog	Double crochet 2 stitches together. Also means to decrease.
27.	dec	Decrease; or decreases, or decreasing
28.	Dtr	Double treble
29.	FL	Front loop (s)
30.	Foll	Follow; or follows; or following
31.	FP	Front post
32.	FPdc	Front post double crochet
33.	FPsc	Front post single crochet
34.	FPtr	Front post triple crochet
35.	G or g	Gram (s) metric weight similar to ounces. 1 g = 0.35 oz.
36.	Hdc	Half double crochet
37.	inc	Increase; or increases; or increasing.
38.	Lp or lps	Loop or loops
39.	M	Meter. 1 meter = 39.37 inches
40.	MC	Main color
41.	mm	Millimeter. 1 mm = .001 meter
42.	oz	Ounce or ounces. 1 oz =28.4 grams
43.	P	Picot (decorative loops formed by ch sts; especially used in Irish lace crochet.
44.	Pat or patt	Pattern or patterns
45.	Pc	Popcorn
46.	P m	Place marker
47.	Prev	Previous

Crochet Abbreviations Basic List
(In Alpha order after the symbols)

	Abbreviations	Descriptions
48.	Rem	Remain; or remaining
49.	REP	Repeat or repeats
50.	Rnd	Round or rounds
51.	RS	Right side, meaning public side of a garment ; or right hand side of an item
52.	Sc	Single crochet
53.	Sc2tog	Single crochet 2 together. This is a type of decrease.
54.	Sk	Skip
55.	Sl st	Slip stitch
56.	Sp or sps	Space or spaces
57.	St or sts	Stitch or stitches
58.	Tch or t-ch	Turning chain
59.	Tbl	Through back loop
60.	Tog	Together
61.	Tr or Trc	Treble crochet
62.	Trtr	Triple treble crochet
63.	WS	Wrong side (inside of a garment)
64.	Yd or yds	Yard or yards
65.	Yo or YO	Yarn over
66.	Yoh	Yarn over hook.

TIP # 63
DIFFERENCE BETWEEN
"AMERICAN" TERMS AND "BRITISH" TERMS.

When you read a crochet pattern purchased outside the United States, take note if the pattern is written as "American Terminology" or "English/British" Terminology. This difference in terminology can be very confusing unless you understand the difference.

- *The first difference is there is NO "single crochet" stitch listed in British terminology.*
- *Second difference, The British call the single crochet stitch "double crochet.*
- *Third, American style, makes the chain stitches at the end of the row, then turn. British style turn the crochet work, then chain at the beginning of the work.*
- *Be consistent. If you always chain, then turn; or you turn work then chain, be consistent.*

American	English	English Abbreviation	Symbol
single crochet	double crochet	DC, dc	+
extended single	extended double	EXDC, exdc	
half double	half treble	HTR, htr	
double	treble	TR, tr	
treble	double treble	DTR, dtr	
double treble	triple treble	TRTR (or TTR), trtr (or ttr)	

Reference: Chart from the *Crochet Stitch Bible* by Betty Barnden, published by Krause Publications, copyright 2004

MY OWN PATTERN READING NOTES

336 Crochet Tips !
The Solutions Book for Crocheters

MY OWN PATTERN READING NOTES

Basic International Crochet Symbols & How to follow a Crochet Schematic Chart

Chapter 7

TIP #64

Outside the U. S. crocheters work with the **international crochet symbol system.** This system was invented by the Japanese in the 1960's or even earlier; however Americans could find the system of crochet if they looked in books published outside of the United States. For many years it was referred to as the JIS (Japanese International Symbol) system. **There are more than 50 of these symbols.**

In 2003, Ms. Janet Tombu of Victoria, British Columbia and I worked on the format for a true type Crochet Symbols Font, which could be loaded onto your computer. Within the computer type font, the 66 basic International symbols are included. The font is used throughout *336 Crochet Tips !*

The premise of the International Crochet Symbol is that if there is only one set of symbols for the whole world, then language does not matter, because the pattern reader need only know the symbols and then "read" the symbols in any language.

TIP #65

By learning the international crochet symbol system, you can crochet a pattern in any language, because the symbols are universal and do not rely upon a language translation. For example, if you travel to Germany and purchase a crochet book, the symbols will be the same even though you may not speak the language.

Once the symbols have been visualized and memorized, they will allow you crochet and read/interpret the pattern at a faster rate.

Tip # 66

Basic Crochet Symbols With American Equivalents

Stitches Used	American Abbreviations	International Crochet Symbol
Chain stitch	Ch	∞∞
Single crochet	Sc	XXX
Half Double Crochet	Hdc	TTT
Double Crochet	Dc	╫╫╫
Triple Crochet	Trc	╪╪╪
Picot	Pic	⊕⊕⊕
Slip Stitch	Sl st	●●●
Crochet symbols in this section provided by Janet Tombu , British Columbia, Canada		

TIPS # 67 - 77

1. A chart shows a pattern as it appears on the public side. Crochet symbol charts are like "maps", which simplify written instructions for pattern stitches, color work and garment shaping.

2. **Read an international Pattern worked in ROWS from the bottom up.**

3. Begin at bottom, right corner if the pattern is written in rows; or find the "1" . *ASSUMPTION: The general assumption is that crochet charts are written for right hand crocheters.* **Recommendation:** Left hand crocheters can purchase transparencies from an office supply store, photocopy the pattern on to the transparency, then simply flip it over and the pattern will be in a direction best for left hand crocheters.

4. Read the chart from right to left on the "public" side row **(Odd numbered rows)**

5. Read **Even numbered rows from left to right** on a non-public side row.

6. For crochet patterns worked in ROUNDS, begin to read the pattern from the center. Recommendation: Find the #1 in the center, this will tell you exactly where to begin a chart pattern.

7. Either one of these symbols mean to "fasten off here": ◁ or ▷

8. Either one of the following symbols mean to "Start here".: ◀, ▶, ▲, ▼.

9. Either one of the following symbols mean "Direction of work": ↵, ∩, ↻.

10. **Right hand crocheters** will always be crocheting toward her left. In a motif or on rounds, she will always be crocheting counter clockwise.

11. Left hand crocheters will always be crocheting to her right. In a motif or on rounds, she will always be crocheting clockwise.

WHAT TO DO AT THE END OF A ROW

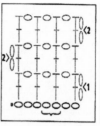 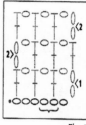

Fig. 1   Fig. 2

Work edge stitches (turning chains) in one of two ways depending on the application you plan to use. Using the Open Stitch Family as an example (Fig. 1), the chart shows the turning chain worked outside of the main body of stitches. For garments, work the turning chains outside the main body of the stitch so that the pattern repeats continuously across seam lines. Fig. 2 shows the turning chain worked within the main body of stitches. When you want even sides on a rectangular piece such as in a blanket, work the turning chain within the main body of stitches. You can convert the patterns in the gallery from one type of turning chain to the other depending on your application.

The above Chart is from : *Donna Kooler's Encyclopedia of Crochet*, **published by Leisure Arts, copyrighted 2003**

TIP # 78

When I work from a chart I always use <u>figure 1.</u> The reasons I use figure 1:

⌘   Method 1 does not leave gapping "holes" along the side of my work.   This is very important in the making of crochet fashions and garments.
⌘   The hole is unsightly and gaudy.
⌘   It does not allow for neat seams and construction.

TIP # 79
Additional Symbol Stitches that can be found in American Patterns

SYMBOL	ABBREVIATION
⭕	CHAIN STITCH
O	TURNING CH
✕	SC (SINGLE CROCHET)
⊤	DOUBLE CROCHET
⊤	TRIPLE CROCHET STITCH
●	SL ST
◈	2 DC, CH 1, 2 DC SHELL
⋔	3 ST DC CLUSTER
⬧	3 ST DC POPCORN
⬥	3 ST HDC POPCORN
⬡	5 STITCH DOUBLE CROCHET POPCORN STITCH

	5 DOUBLE CROCHET SHELL STITCH
	5 ST HDC POPCORN
	BACK POST DC
	BACK POST HDC
	SC IN BACK LOOP ONLY
	BACK POST SC
	BACK POST TRIPLE CROCHET
	BOUILLON STITCH
	CLOSED PICOT
	DC 2 TOG (DOUBLE CROCHET 2 TOGETHER)
	DC 3 TOG (DOUBLE CROCHET 3 STITCHES TOGETHER)
	DC 4 TOG (DOUBLE CROCHET 4 STITCHES TOGETHER)
	DC IN BACK LOOP
	DOUBLE CROCHET INCREASE BY 1 MORE STITCH
	DOUBLE CROCHET LOOP STITCH

	EXTENDED SC
	FRONT POST DC
	FRONT POST HDC
	FRONT POST SC
	FRONT POST TRIPLE CROCHET
	HDC 2 TOG
	HDC 3 STITCHES TOG (DECREASE BY 2 MORE STITCHES)
	HDC INCREASE BY 1 MORE STITCH
	HDC INCREASE BY 2 STITCHES
	DOUBLE CROCHET INC BY 1 MORE
	INVERTED "Y" STITCH
	OMEGA LACE CROCHET
	OPEN PICOT
	SC 2 TOG
	SC 3 TOG (SINGLE 3 STITCHES TOG)

336 Crochet Tips !
The Solutions Book for Crocheters

⋊	SC CRAB ST OR REVERSE SC (WORK WILL BE FROM LEFT TO RIGHT)
ᐻ	SC INCREASE BY 1
ᐺ	SC INCREASE BY 2 MORE STITCHES
⋈	SC LOOP ST
Ⱥ	TRC 3 TOG (TRIPLE CROCHET DECREASE BY 2 STITCHES)
Ⱥ	TRIPLE CROCHET 2 TOG
⋨	TRIPLE CROCHET CROSSOVER STITCH
V	TRIPLE CROCHET INCREASE BY 1 MORE ST
W	TRIPLE CROCHET INCREASE BY 2 MORE
Ï	TRIPLE CROCHET IN BACK LOOP
Y	Y STITCH

NOTES ABOUT
INTERNATIONAL SYMBOL CROCHET

336 Crochet Tips !
The Solutions Book for Crocheters

Hook Basics & Storing Hooks

Chapter 8

Tips # 80

Hooks come in 2 formats: rounded headed hooks and inline "Flat headed" hooks. In Round-headed hooks, the hooks sit above the stem; for example, The Boye/Wrights brand of crochet hook. On Inline hooks, the hook is "in line" with the stem of the hook; for example, The Susan Bates brand of crochet hook.

Tip 81

Keep your **crochet hooks,** in a case or travel toothbrush holder to prevent them from getting chips, nicks, unwanted grooves.

Tip #82

Nicks will cause yarn to snag and unravel.

Tip # 83

The best place for your crochet hooks is in a container within your crochet kit , bag or tote.

Tip # 84

Hooks designed **primarily use for yarn** are categorized with alphabets and metric. For example: **size H is 5.00mm**

Tip # 85

Yarn hooks range in size from letter B (the smallest—2.25mm) to letter Q (the largest 15.00mm). The metric equivalent for yarn hooks range from 2.25 mm to 19.00mm.

Tip # 86

Steel hooks are primarily used for threads and very fine yarns. **Steel hooks use a numeric system of categorizing**. For example: #14 is .75mm by Boye/Wrights; however #14 is .70mm by Susan Bates. (See **Hooks Chart**)

Tip # 87

Steel hooks range in size from **.60mm to 3.50 mm in metric sizes. 14 (the smallest) to 00 (the largest.)** These hooks will make a very tight stitch as opposed to its yarn-hook equivalent.

Tip # 88

For clarity, it is best to learn the metric equivalent of the hook you want to use. Each manufacturer of hooks have different numbers for the same metric equivalent.

Tip # 89

▶▶Warning! ◀◀
Not all manufacturers of hooks sold in the U. S. A. use the same size letter or number to represent the equivalent metric size. While Susan Bates hooks are made in Mexico, the company refers to its hooks as "American". Please see the comparison on the International Hooks Chart.

Tip # 90

The best hooks are made of aluminum or steel. However for travel, it is best to use plastic or wooden hooks. NOTE: if working on a thread project, understand that there are no small plastic or wooden hooks.

Tip # 91

When purchasing plastic or acrylic hooks, inspect for rough and jagged edges. These types of edges will create snags and splitting of yarns.

Tip # 92

The size of the hook and the thickness of the yarn, along with how tightly or loosely you work, determines the size of the stitches, which is called what is referred to as GAUGE.

TIP # 93

✠   There are six types of crochet hooks: 1) ordinary yarn hooks in sizes B – Q; 2) Steel or thread crochet hooks--.60mm to 3.50mm; 3) Afghan or Tunisian hooks; 4) Double-ended or Cro-hooks; 5) Quick or jumbo hooks; 6) flexi-afghan hooks.

TIP # 94

✠   Afghan or Tunisian hook is from 9 to 14 inches in length.   It has a crochet hook on one end, and a knitting knob on the other. This type of hook is used to work a type of crochet which is tightly woven and similar to knitting called to Afghan or Tunisian crochet.

TIP # 95

✠   Double-ended or Cro-Hook has a crochet hook on each end. It is from 9- to 14-inches in length.   This type of hook creates a form of Afghan or Tunisian crochet, which can be worked in two different colors and reversible.   This hook is also used to create Omega Lace Crochet. (See the book: FABULOUS CROCHETED PONCHOS by Terry Taylor, Published by Lark Books)

TIP # 96

✠   Flexible Afghan or Tunisian Hook has a nylon cable attached. This cable is from 20 to 36 inches long; and is used for large projects.

TIP #97

✠   "Quick" hooks are sized from L – S (7.00mm – 19.00mm) are used to work two or three crochet yarns together.   These hooks are usually made of plastic or acrylic.   Be sure to inspect the hooks for rough edges.   Crochet is worked very large and can be worked very fast.

TIP # 98

✠   There are 2 tools, which can be complements to regular crochet hooks: 1) Hairpin loom—which creates "hairpin lace crochet"; and 2) jumbo knitting needle—which creates "Broomstick lace" crochet.

TIP # 99

Hairpin Loom or fork is used to work Hairpin Lace Crochet or Maltese lace crochet. The "loom" or "fork" is an adjustable tool, which can create hairpin lace from 2 inches to 6 inches wide. In Europe, the tool is a "hairpin" **(Π)** looking item. Each size has its own "hairpin" **. This loom or fork is worked in tandem with an ordinary crochet hook. The stitches are formed by spinning the loom/ fork/ pin.**

TIP # 100

The broomstick lace pin is usually a knitting needle is size 19, 35 (inch in diameter) , or 50 (1-inch in diameter). This is comparable to 25mm to 35mm in size. The large knit-pin is worked with the pin in the tension or opposite hand and the crochet hook in the dominant hand.

International Hooks Chart

Chapter 9

TIP # 101

Each manufacturer of crochet hooks is allowed to create their own system for numbering the crochet hooks. This creates a major issue for crocheters—who do not know there is a major difference in crochet hooks.

TIP # 102

The designer may have worked the pattern in a "round-headed" hook, but the publisher uses the "flat-head" hooks in the printed matter or vis-à-vis. Be aware!! *Read and know* the difference between round-headed hook measurements and in-line hook measurements. Please refer to the hooks chart at the end of this chapter

TIP # 103

Each hook can be compared to comparable sizes and manufacturers.

TIP # 104

"Metric" is the golden rule of measurement. While the United States is not "officially" using metric measurements, Metric measurements are showing up on all U.S. products; and crochet hooks are no different.

- ✓ Find the metric size using the left side of the chart
- ✓ Find the name of the manufacturer on the hook
- ✓ Compare the sizes.

TIP # 105

There are "yarn hooks" and "thread hooks". Yarn hooks will always have an alphabet on them.

For example, "H/8 5.00mm). The "H" indicates that this hook is to be used for yarn. The "5.00mm" is the Metric size. The "/8" system is used only by the British; also knitters may use this number as an equivalent to knitting needle size. Yarn hooks are from "B" (2.25mm) to "K" (6.50mm) in the basic crochet kit. There are larger alpha sized hooks.

TIP # 106

Thread hooks have a series of numbers. For example, "3 and 2.10mm". The first number indicates that this hook is used for working with crochet thread and was based on an "Imperial system".

The "2.10mm" indicates the metric size of the hook. Thread hooks are sized from "16", which about ".50mm" (extremely fine hook) to the largest "00", which is "3.50mm".

The number matches with the thread numbering system. For example, #100 thread is very fine, while #3 thread is very large.

TIP #107
THE INTERNATIONAL HOOKS CHART

1. Look on your hook, see what the size is in the Metric "mm" and which alphabet is imprinted on it.
2. If it is a yarn hook there will also be an "alphabet" from "B" to "Q". While the majority of hooks purchased in America indicate an alphabet on them, there are few, which do not have an alphabet, therefore rely on the metric equivalent.
3. Look on the chart. See The name of the manufacturer from the hook. Find the exact metric size on the hooks chart. For example the yarn hook may state the following: "H/8 5.00mm Boye/Wrights". First go find the section that says "Boye/Wrights" on the hooks chart. Second, go find the Letter "H", then find the metric "mm", which would be "5.0mm" . You can then compare the Boye Wrights hook to all the similar hooks in that size range on the hooks chart.
4. Crochet hooks also carry the knitting needle equivalent to help knitters recognize an equal size to their needles. For example, H/8 5.00mm. The number 8 indicates that the H crochet hook will be similar in size to the #8 knitting needle.

Metric Equal	Boye-Wrights Made in USA		Susan Bates Made in Mexico		Caron	Clover & Takumi Made in Japan		Skacel & Addi Made in Germany	
	Yarn Hooks	Steel Thread Hooks [1]	Yarn Hooks	Steel Thread hooks	Yarn Hooks	Yarn Hooks	Steel Thread Hooks	Yarn Hooks	Thread Hooks
0.60									.60 [2]
0.70		14 [2]		14 [2]			.70 [2]		
0.75		14 [2]							0.75
0.85		13							
0.90				13			0.90		
1.00		12		12			1.00		1.00
1.05				11			1.05		
1.10		11							
1.15				10			1.15		
1.25				9			1.25		1.25
1.30		10							
1.40		9		8			1.40		
1.50		8		7			1.50		1.50

336 Crochet Tips !
The Solutions Book for Crocheters

Metric Equal	Boye-Wrights Made in USA Yarn Hooks	Boye-Wrights Made in USA Steel Thread Hooks ¹	Susan Bates Made in Mexico Yarn Hooks	Susan Bates Made in Mexico Steel Thread hooks	Caron Yarn Hooks	Clover & Takumi Made in Japan Yarn Hooks	Clover & Takumi Made in Japan Steel Thread Hooks	Skacel & Addi Made in Germany Yarn Hooks	Skacel & Addi Made in Germany Thread Hooks
1.60				6			1.60		
1.65		7							
1.70				5			1.70		
1.75				4			1.75		1.75
1.80		6							
1.90		5							
2.00		4							2.00
2.10		3		3			2.10		
2.20				2			2.20		
2.25	B	2	B		B				
2.35				1			2.35		
2.50						B		B	2.50
2.55				0			2.55		
2.70				00			2.70		
2.75	C	1	C		C	C			
3.00		0				D			3.00
3.25	D		D		D				3.25

336 Crochet Tips !
The Solutions Book for Crocheters

Metric Equal	Boye-Wrights Made in USA Yarn Hooks	Boye-Wrights Made in USA Steel Thread Hooks [1]	Susan Bates Made in Mexico Yarn Hooks	Susan Bates Made in Mexico Steel Thread hooks	Caron Yarn Hooks	Clover & Takumi Made in Japan Yarn Hooks	Clover & Takumi Made in Japan Steel Thread Hooks	Skacel & Addi Made in Germany Yarn Hooks	Skacel & Addi Made in Germany Thread Hooks
3.50	E	OO	E		E	E		3.50	
3.75	F		F		F	F		.3.75	
4.00			G		G	G		4.00	
4.25	G		G		7				
4.50	7		7					4.50	
5.00	H		H		H	H		5.00	
5.50	I		I		I	I		5.50	
6.00	J		J		J	J		6.00	
6.50	K		K		K	K			
7.00	L							7.00	
8.00	M		L					8.00	
9.00	N		M					9.00	
10.00	P		N					10.00	
11.00									
12.00			P					12.00	

[1] Thread hooks will make a very tight stitch as opposed to its yarn hook equivalent.

[2] This is the number shown on the hook.

MY CROCHET HOOK TIPS !
MY SOLUTIONS

Yarn Basics

Chapter 10

336 Crochet Tips !
The Solutions Book for Crocheters

TIP # 108
Understanding the Yarn Label

There are many types and classes of yarns. However, your best reference guide is to read the Yarn's label. *A good yarn label should provide you with EVERYTHING YOU NEED TO KNOW before you make an investment in the yarn.*

Here is a great example of the information the yarn label should have:

TIP # 109
There are 13 listings
on a great yarn label:

1. **Name of the company who made the yarn.**
2. **How to get in touch so that you can communicate with them if you have problems.**
3. **Country of origin; so that you can be cognizant of animal rights laws or problems, especially if you hear news of how bad the sheep or goats are treated in a particular country. This has an effect on the quality of the yarn.**

4. Yarn Name.
5. Yarn content, example how much wool; acrylic, nylon and the percentage of each type of content.
6. The Class of the yarn in the old system, for example DK or Sport Weight.
7. Yarn should be listed in both weights of measure: American Units (for example, pounds and ounces) and in Metric Units (for example Kilograms and grams).
8. The Length of the yarn should also be imprinted on the label in both American Units (for example: inches and yards) and in Metric Units (for example centimeters and meters) whether the yarn is wrapped as "pull skein", "ball" or "hank".
9. How to launder and care for the yarn. A great label has both the international laundry symbols and the American word translation, so there is no doubt how the yarn manufacturer wants you to take care of yarn—after a lot of time is invested in creating a crochet item.
10. Color and Dye lot codes. When yarn is manufactured, there is a formula to create the exact color you purchased. Each time the yarn manufacturer changes the formula a new dye lot is assigned to the label. Each time, the color is varies slightly. So you have to be sure that you check to be sure that you are purchasing all of the same "Color and Dye Lot Codes". If you fail to check you will have slight color variations in your item.
11. Recommended crochet hook or knitting needle in the American Alpha system and in the Metric system.
12. The label should list 2 gauges: The horizontal gauge, which tells how many STITCHES to the inch/cm; and the vertical gauge which tells how many ROWS to the inch/cm.
13. Inventory tracking Universal Product Code (UPC).

TIP # 110
Need to Know The Following About Yarns

Without the sensation of the touch of yarns, many crocheters would be lost for an art to muse with. There are several things you *N-E-E-D T-O K-N-O-W*.

Publishers, and crochet designers/writers have to **ASSUME** you know certain basics or they would spend countless pages in a book about a given technique just explaining yarns.   So here are the basics:

1. When learning to crochet or working on a new pattern stitch, **practice in a light or bright colored yarn**. This helps the eyes "see" where the hook is going.

2. **Dark colors use more yarn**.   Therefore, when crocheting with dark colors, purchase at least one more skein than the pattern requires.

3. **Yarns can be spun from natural fibers**. Yarns can be made of many different materials. There are natural **animal** (protein) based fibers: wool, alpaca, mohair, angora, cashmere, qivut (Alaskan Musk Ox), Himalayan Yak, or camel. **Natural cellulose** (plant) fibers, which come from plants such as cotton, linen, flax, bamboo, soy, corn. There are natural fibers which come **directly from insects** such as the cultivated Bombyx Mori worm which produces silk or the wild bombyx mori , which produces tussah (a more rough type of silk usually natural brown).

4. **Synthetic fibers are man-made**. Many yarns are blends of several different fibers, both natural and synthetic. Acrylic is the most common of synthetic yarns and one of the most economical. In worsted weight form it is very heavy for crocheters.

5. RECOMMENDATION: **An excellent book to learn about fibers is called *Beyond Wool*, by Candace Eisner Strick, and published by *Martingale & Company*.**

6. Some yarns come in hanks. **A hank of yarn**, means that the yarn has not been commercially placed into a "pull skein". A hank is twisted. Once it is untwisted, it is then loosely tied into large ring. This ring must then be gently wound into a ball **before** you crochet.

7. When working with **novelty yarns**, be sure to purchase one skein or ball or hank to see whether you like crocheting with the yarn. The finished texture of the yarn may have quite an unusual feel in your hands. Sometimes novelty yarns drag and pull at a different tension, which you are accustomed to.

8. **Some yarns may not be pulled** or ripped out once you crochet them; for example, mohair is very difficult to pull out. By purchasing a practice ball first, you can play with a combination of stitches.

9. Be sure to **follow the manufacturer's recommendation** for laundry care. The way that you care for the yarn is in international symbols on the yarn label (See the cards on 'Laundry Care". Also see cards on reading the "Yarn Labels"

10. **The Term "Weight" refers to the thickness or thinness of a yarn.** Commercial yarn is sold in several different thicknesses or "weights". All these yarns can also consist of "plys" which does not affect the weight category of the yarn. A "ply" is merely a strand of yarn twisted upon another. For example, "2 ply" means two strands were twisted together to make one strand of yarn. Ply and weight are not related terms.

11. **Lace Weight Yarn:** This type of yarn is primarily used by crocheters to create crochet lace; The yarn's properties are as fine as #3 or #5 Crochet thread. This weight also includes all levels of crochet threads. (See Chapter on "Thread Basics") **Class 0 on the yarn label.**

12. **Baby Weight Yarn:** On the label you will see "Baby" or "Fingering Yarn". This size yarn is more commonly used for baby items or lightweight summer wear. **Class 1 yarn.**

13. **Baby Sport Yarn:**   You may also see "Baby Sport" on the label. This yarn is just a bit thicker than baby weight and is best for children's fashions. **Class 1 yarn.**

14. **Sock Weight Yarn:**   This yarn is used for making all types of socks.   Sock weight yarn is fine and durable.   It also contains a percentage of wool.   In order to make socks, there must be a percentage of wool or wool-type (fur based) fiber blended into the yarn. **Class 1 yarn**.

15. **Sport-Weight Yarn**: This yarn is twice as thick as baby-weight yarn.   This yarn is excellent for children's clothing, and also for lighter weight garments for crochet fashions.   Depending upon the fiber content, this type of yarn can be used year round. **Class 2 OR Class 3 yarn.**

> In this same category of yarns, you will also find **large crochet threads** from size # 3 (the largest) to size # 8. These threads can be just a soft as yarns.   **Class 2 yarn.**

14. **Double Knitting Yarn:** Also known as "DK" or "Fashion weight" yarn.   This yarn is an "in-between" yarn, since it is heavier than sport weight yet lighter than worsted weight yarn. It is sometimes called "Light Worsted Weight."   Some "microfiber" yarns fall into this category. **Class 3 yarn.**

15. **Worsted-Weight Yarn:** This yarn is twice as thick as sport weight yarn.   This is the most common weight used.   It is an excellent size yarn for beginners. The most popular items to make with this yarn size is afghans, heavy coats, and stuffed toys. It is not a good yarn for "fashions" because it is too bulky.   In warm climates it is definitely not the best choice for a project. "Aran" or "Fisherman" weight yarns fall into this category.   These two types of yarns are made of 100% percent "wool" or other fur-based fibers. **Class 4 yarn.**

16. Bulky Weight Yarn: This weight is excellent for quick projects. It is twice as thick as worsted weight yarn. Many "Craft" weight yarns and "rug" yarns fall into this category. **These yarns may be coarse, hard, scratchy—be careful when working them into garments. Class 5 yarn.**

17. Gigantic-Weight Yarn: Gigantic weight yarn is the thickest yarn and often consists of several yarns put together. It is twice as thick as bulky weight. **Class 6 Yarn.**

18. UNDERSTANDING QUALITY AND EXCELLENCE: Quality yarns stand up to wear; they can e remodeled, some yarns can be pulled out (except perhaps mohair) and re-crocheted.
Quality is a skill acquired mainly through touch and experience. Cost is not a reliable criteria although quality is not "cheap.

TIP # 111

⌘   **Learn to Read the Yarn Label .**

⌘   **Learn the FEEL of the yarn.**

⌘   **Quality work is crucial. Crochet fashions of high quality materials poorly constructed, poorly finished and poorly fitted are a total waste of time and effort.**

⌘   **Take time to match hook size to yarn**

⌘   **Make a good size practice swatch of about 4" x 4" or even larger. The larger, the better up to 8" by 8"**

⌘   **Stitches should not be too loose nor too tight.**

⌘   **Quality material and quality workmanship produce a pleasure and a satisfaction for the crocheter that is as soul soothing and meditation, or a cool drink on a hot summer's day.**

⌘   **Once crochet basics have been mastered through quality, this contributes to QUALITY OF LIFE! And quality of life reduces stress.**

Tip # 112
Simple Substitutions for Yarn Equivalents
Simple Substitutions for Yarn Equivalents is key when you want to crochet a pattern.

Basic Rules of Yarn Substitution

Preferences are key in crocheting. Sometimes you prefer one yarn or color over another. Or, sometimes, you just can't find the yarn mentioned in a pattern.

1. Make a practice swatch in the yarn you want to use; and with the hook which is comfortable for you; approximately 25 stitches wide and 7-10 rows high.
2. If a pattern calls for Yarn A, but you want to use Yarn B, here is the **basic rule** of yarn substitution, for example, the pattern calls for worsted weight yarn, but you like the sport weight color. You can use two strands of sport weight yarn to equal 1 strand of worsted.
3. Here are the equivalents:

Number of Strands *s = Strand; or strands of yarn to work as one strand	Equals =	Recommended Yarn Hooks
2 strands fingering/baby weight	1 strand sport weight	3.50 mm -- 4.25 mm (E to G)
2 *s sport weight	1 strand of worsted weight	3.75 mm -- 5.00 mm (F to H)
2 *s worsted	1 *s of bulky weight	5.50 mm — 6.50 mm (I to K)
3 *s of worsted	1 *s of chunky	6.50 mm—10.00 mm (K to P)

TIP # 113
YARN TYPES & CATEGORIES

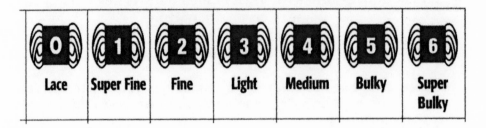

On the new yarn labels, you will see one of the above number types on the yarn label.

Yarn comes in 7 classes. Several years ago, yarns were classified by weight only; however the Craft Yarn Council of America has established a new standard for yarn types.

TIP # 114
YARN CHART ON NEXT PAGE

The types listed below described on the yarn label
Read the chart vertically by class

Yarn category name→	Class 1 Super Fine	Class 2 Fine	Class 3 Light	Class 4 Medium	Class 5 Bulky/Chunky	Class 6 Super Bulky
Type & weight of yarns in Category	Sock, Fingering, Baby	Sport Size 5 crochet thread. (*See "Crochet Threads")	Microfiber, DK (Double Knitting), Light Size 3 crochet thread	Worsted; Afghan; Aran	Chunky; Craft Yarn; Rug Yarn	Bulky; Roving
Suggested Hook sizes in American and Metric Sizes	B – E 2.25 mm - 3.5 mm	E – G [2] 3.5 - 4.5mm	G – I 4.25 - 5.5mm	I – K 5.5 - 6.5 mm	K – M 6.5 - 9 mm	M & larger 9mm and larger
Crochet Gauge based on 4" [3]	21-32 stitches worked in single crochet [3]	16 – 20 stitches worked in single crochet [3]	12 – 17 stitches worked in single crochet [3]	11-14 stitches worked in single crochet [3]	8 – 11 stitches worked in single crochet [3]	5 – 9 stitches worked in single crochet [3]

[1] Metric hook sizes are becoming the "industry standard".

[2] NOTE: Not all hook manufacturers use the same size for the "G" hook. Some manufacturers use "7" to represent the 4.5mm. Recommendation: Read your hook carefully. See Hook Chart in Chapter 9

[3] This gauge will change dramatically if any other crochet stitch is used. Recommendation: Always crochet a sample or practice swatch to check the number of stitches and rows within 4 inches using the hook you have chosen with the yarn you have chosen.

Tip #115
Natural Yarn Fiber Content

Yarns are produced in several types of natural and chemical based fibers. NOTE: It is best to stick with brands that consistently market quality materials:

⌘   **Wool:**   "Wool" is the general name given to all fur-based yarns; however there is a major difference in touch and "handle" of these yarns. Some wools are fine spun from a longer strand and are less likely to pill. Wool holds its shape well.

⌘   **Merino Wool:** is soft and smooth. It wears very well and last a long time.

⌘   **Cashmere:**   is soft, smooth costly and does not wear well. The yarn tends to collect "pill balls".

⌘   **Alpaca:** Comes from the Alpaca family of mammals, which are prevalent in South America. This yarn can be warmer than wool, and is durable.

⌘   **Camel:** soft, smooth and wears extremely well.
Plant make excellent yarns, such as :

⌘   **Cotton:** Plant based fiber. It is both cool and warm. Cotton shrinks and stretches. This oxymoron, may create a problem for some crochet yarns. READ THE LABEL. Mercerized cotton is best for crochet. Cotton blends bring out the best of cotton by not allowing it to shrink or stretch too much.

⌘   **Linen:** Comes from the flax plant. Linen is a "cool" fiber, in that once an item is crocheted, the wearer will remain cool. It is an excellent yarn for the summer.

MY CROCHET TIPS !
MY SOLUTIONS

End Of the Row: What To Do

Chapter 11

336 Crochet Tips !
The Solutions Book for Crocheters

TIP # 116

One of the most confusing things for crocheters is figuring out where the very last stitch is located.

Here are some recommendations to help solve this problem:

1. **Be Consistent** with where you put the hook into the last stitch.

2. **Count the stitches in the row!** As soon as you complete the last stitch of a row, if you are not sure then *COUNT THE STITCHES IN THE ROW*! There is no substitute or shortcut for accuracy. **Accuracy is a form of quality control; and quality always bring positive results.**

3. **Turning chains:** At the end of a row, you will have to make additional chains to give the necessary stitch height to begin next row. These additional chains are called "turning chains". Some patterns will want you to *"use the turning chain as the first stitch"*. My preference is NOT to use the turning chain as the first stitch, because sometimes there is a gap created by using the turning chain as a first stitch. So, I would rather have a little bulk on the edge of row, then use the turning chain to anchor the edging. Therefore, add 1 more stitch to the count to keep your stitch count according to the designers count.

4. **After making the turning chain:** turn work around from left to right (Left Hander: turns from right to left), until the "Wrong side" or opposite side is facing you.

5. **Place a small marker in the last stitch:** As soon as you make the last stitch on a row, then place a small marker on safety pin into that stitch. Leave the marker in the stitch until you complete the next row above it. When you come to this marker again, you will know that this is the last stitch, and you will have to work into it, so that you count will remain the same.

Tɪᴘ # 117
The Number of Chain Stitches
to turn your work:

International Crochet Symbol	Turning Chains	American Stitch Name
Crochet symbols in this section provided by Knitware ᵗᵐ, British Columbia, Canada as a crochet symbols font.		
XXX	O	Sc uses 1 ch to turn
TTTTT	O O	Hdc uses 2 chs to turn
朿朿朿	O O O	Dc uses 3 chs to turn (**NOTE: Sometimes you can use 2 chs to turn to make the edges straighter**)
朿朿朿	O O O O	Tr uses 4 chs to turn

336 Crochet Tips !
The Solutions Book for Crocheters

TIP # 118

⌘   **A crochet pattern chart shows the "graphics" or "Schematic" of a pattern as it appears on the public side.** This means that when you look at the right-hand side of the schematic, it will be odd numbered rows and start on right-hand side of the crochet work.

⌘   **Left hand side of the pattern schematic will start in even-numbered rows and the finished product is on the non-public side of the crochet fabric, known as the "wrong side of the fabric".**

⌘   **Crochet symbol charts are like "maps",** which simplify written instructions for pattern stitches, color work and garment shaping.

⌘   **Read Row-styled Patterns from the bottom up**. Begin at bottom, right corner if the pattern is written in rows; or find the "1"

⌘   **Read the chart from right to left** on the "public" side row **(Odd numbered rows)**

⌘   **Read Even numbered rows from left to right** on a wrong side row.

⌘   **You can even transfer the crochet chart to a transparency and simply flip the transparency at the end of the row, so that you have a visual document to work with to assist with understanding the pattern.**

⌘   This method is especially good for left-hand crocheters. If the pattern is on a transparency for the left hand crocheter, she would begin by flipping the transparency, so that the pattern begins on her left.

Tip #118

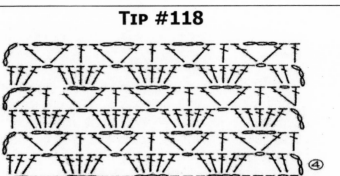

Above (↑↑) graphics is from a Japanese Crochet Book

Here is an example of a simple pattern with turning chains included:

Graphics below (↓↓;) is from *Crochet Fantasy Magazine*.

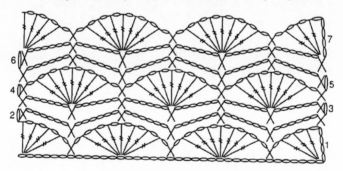

REDUCED SAMPLE OF PATTERN

60 ♦ CROCHET FANTASY

Skill Levels
&
Metric Conversions

Chapter 12

TIP # 119
Crochet Patterns are rated

Crochet patterns are commercially rated by the Craft Yarn Council of America yarn standards.   This rating is based upon surveys of crocheters,   who have submitted questions to magazines and book publishers.

SKILL LEVELS FOR CROCHET

1	▣☐☐☐	**Beginner**	Projects for first-time crocheters using basic stitches. Minimal shaping.
2	▣▣☐☐	**Easy**	Projects using yarn with basic stitches, repetitive stitch patterns, simple color changes, and simple shaping and finishing.
3	▣▣▣☐	**Intermediate**	Projects using a variety of techniques, such as basic lace patterns or color patterns, mid-level shaping and finishing.
4	▣▣▣▣	**Experienced**	Projects with intricate stitch patterns, techniques and dimension, such as non-repeating patterns, multi-color techniques, fine threads, small hooks, detailed shaping and refined finishing.

Above graphic is from the Craft Yarn Council of America

TIP # 120
Metric Conversions

While the rest of the world has been on the metric system, the U. S. just beginning to use this decimal based math system. It seems as though it is just one more thing to remember; however, the conversion can be more accurate than our fraction-based system.

To Convert:			
To Convert from	To Get:	Multiply by	Formula Example
Inches ["]	Cm	2.54	7" x 2.54 = 17.18 cm
Centimeters [cm]	In. ["]	0.394	21 cm x 0.394 = 8.27"
Yards [yds]	m	0.914	4 yds x 0.914 = 3.66 m
Meters [m]	Yds	1.093	5 m x 1.093 = 5.47 yds
Ounces [oz]	G	28.35	12 oz x 28.35 = 340.20 g
Grams [g]	oz	.035	220 g x .035 = 7.7 oz

TIP # 121

Here is the basic fractions conversions chart used by crocheters. **Chart is from:** *I Taught Myself to Crochet* booklet by the Boye Wrights Company

METRIC EQUIVALENTS

Comparison of ounces (oz.) and grams (gm.)
(slightly rounded off)

oz.	½	1	1½	1¾	2	2½	3	3½	4
gm.	14	28	42	50	57	71	85	100	113

Comparison of inches (in.) and centimeters (cm.)
(slightly rounded off)

in.	¼	½	¾	1	2	3	4	5	6	7	8
cm.	0.6	1.3	2	2.5	5	8	10	13	15	18	20

in.	9	10	11	12	13	14	15	16	17	18
cm.	23	26	28	31	33	36	38	41	43	46

in.	19	20	21	22	23	24	25	26	27	28
cm.	48	51	53	56	58	61	64	66	69	71

in.	29	30	31	32	33	34	35	36	37	38
cm.	74	76	79	81	84	86	89	91	94	97

in.	39	40	41	42	43	44	45	46	47	48
cm.	99	102	104	107	109	112	114	117	119	122

NOTE: if you need more ounces or inches shown, either add two of the given numerals together or use the following multiplication

Thread Crochet Basics
&
Steel Hooks

Chapter 13

TIP # 122

Thread Crochet Basics

1. The higher the thread number, for example size # 50, the finer the thread.   The Lower the number, for example size # 3, the more coarse the thread.

2. Thread crochet works best with steel crochet hooks.   Good steel hooks have a strong pull when a magnet is placed near it.

3. Some thread crochet hooks are made of nickel or other alloys; and these will not be magnetic.

4. You may prefer to work with your finer yarn hooks, such as B (2.25mm), C (2.75), or D (3.25).   These hooks will yield a much larger stitch pattern.   Some crocheters prefer yarn hooks to steel hooks because, for example Boye/Wrights, yarn hooks a longer and do not press into the palm of the hand like steel hooks, which are only 5 inches long.

5. Keep in mind that your individual crocheting style may call for a slightly larger or smaller hook or a thicker or thinner crochet cotton thread than the one which is recommended for a specific project.

6. Be careful not to grip the thread too tightly if you wrap thread with the little finger of the tension hand, or you could find your have tensed the muscles in your arm, which will become very sore.

7. Mercerized cotton: Most cotton used for lace crochet has an additional finish called mercerization.   This is a chemical process which strengthens the cotton threads, and adds a sheen or luster. This caustic process also prevents dyed cottons from fading, which is the nature of cotton. A mercerized cotton is difficult to dye;

however it can be successfully dyed using a vinegar-water based solution. Mercerized cotton is ideal for heirloom crochet.

8. Fine thread or lace crochet may need blocking. **There are two methods of blocking: Heat and chemical**. Both methods cause the crochet thread/lace project to look better. For threads other than cotton, you may prefer a chemical blocking. *[NOTE: BE SURE TO TEST THE CHEMICAL ON THE GAUGE SWATCH BEFORE USING IT. SYNTHETIC THREADS MAY CHANGE COLOR OR HAVE SOME OTHER REACTION]* . Chemical blocking is a type of solution that comes with starch or without starch. The solution without starch is a "Non-Starch" Spray. For cotton threads, a mild heat blocking may be necessary for the item maintain and hold its finished shaping..

TIP #123

UNDERSTANDING QUALITY AND EXCELLENCE: Quality threads stand up to wear; they can be remodeled and re-crocheted. Quality is a skill acquired mainly through touch and experience. Cost is not a reliable criteria although quality is not "cheap".

⌘   **Learn to Read the Thread Label .**
⌘   **Learn the FEEL of the thread. Each type of thread has a different feel in your tension hand.**
⌘   **Quality work is crucial. Crochet fashions of high quality materials poorly constructed, poorly finished and poorly fitted are a total waste of time and effort.**
⌘   **Take time to match hook size to thread size.**
⌘   **Make a good size practice swatch of about 4" x 4"**
⌘   **Stitches should not be too loose nor too tight. In thread crochet, stitches, which are too loose will cause the item to be misshapened and will not have a cohesive uniform look. This cohesive uniform look is what people admire about Thread crocheted items.   Stitches which are too tight with cause the item to look "cramped".**
⌘   **Quality material and quality workmanship produce a pleasure and a satisfaction for the crocheter that is as soul**

soothing and meditation, or a cool drink on a hot summer's day.

⌘ Once crochet basics have been mastered through quality, this contributes to QUALITY OF LIFE! And quality of life reduces stress.

TIP # 124
Types of Threads Used for Crochet

There are many types of crochet threads on the market, such as mercerized cotton (The most popular type); linen; silk, bamboo, soy and synthetics such as lurex.

Here is a description of the most common crochet cottons with their   approximate yardage, and a chart of hook size equivalents.

Fiber Name	Comes From	Properties	Durability
Cotton	Cotton plant, the bolls are used	Non-resilient	Moderately durable
Bamboo	Bamboo plant. Stalks are used	Non-resilient	Very durable
Linen & Flax	Flax Plant (Linen is the center portion of the plant— Flax is the outer portion of the plant	Non-resilient as a thread	Very durable & projects are cool to wear.
Soy	Soy plant	Non resilient	Very durable
Silk	Bombyx Mori worm.	Very resilient	Warm and durable

Fiber Name	Comes From	Properties	Durability
	Cocoon is used before the worm hatches		
Synthetic	Range of contents	Resilient depending upon the chemical make up	Durability depends upon the way yarn is spun. For example cabled spun is stronger than twisted spun.

TIP # 125

The Higher the thread number, for example size # 50, the finer the thread. The Lower the number, for example size # 3, the more coarse the thread.

TIP # 126

Threads are in a range of sizes just like yarns.

There are natural threads in Cotton, Linen, Bamboo, Soy, Silk.

There are also, synthetic threads, such as lurex, blending filaments.

TIP #127

Recommended: that steel hooks be used for thread projects. They create a more tighter stitch, than with yarn hooks. The larger thread hook sizes, for example 00, 0, and 1 may be used with yarn project such as toys; handbags, and hats where a tight stitch is needed.

TIP #128
SEE CHART ON NEXT PAGE

Thread Crochet Basics for Steel Hooks

SECTION 13

Thread Category	Super Fine Thread 220 - 324 yds [1]	Fine Thread Weight 174 - 216 yds	Light Weight thread 124 - 174 yds	Med. Weight Thread 111 - 124 yds	Bulky Weight Thread 83 - 124 yds
Thread Size -> NOTE: The higher the number, the finer the thread	# 60 #50 #40	# 30 # 20	# 15 # 12 # 10	# 8 # 5	# 5 #3
Recommended Gauge [1] in dc, based upon 3" by 3" area	52 – 45 stitches and 22–18 rows	47 – 40 stitches and 19 – 16 rows	40—36 stitches and 17—14 rows	35—30 stitches and 15—12 rows	32—25 stitches and 13–10 rows
Recommended Hook in metric size range [2]	.60 – 1.30 mm	1.05–1.80 mm	1.25–2.10 mm	1.40–2.50 mm	2.00–3.25 mm
Recommend: Hook in U. S. Size Range	10 -- 14**	6 - 11	3 -- 9	1 -- 8	0 - 4

Recommended: that steel hooks be used for thread projects. They create a more tighter stitch, than with yarn hooks.

[1] NOTE: The gauge used was based on a 3 " by 3 " sample square These amounts are approximate. Check accuracy via your gauge/practice swatch.

[2] There are major discrepancies in hook sizes between U. S. manufacturers of crochet hooks. It is recommended to purchase hooks with metric measurements for accuracy. See Hook Chart Section of CROCHET TIPS !

** American hooks are sized as 14 as the smallest/finest hooks while 3.50 is the largest of the steel hooks. Zero hook is really larger than "4"

The Higher the thread number, for example size # 50, the finer the thread. The Lower the number, for example size # 3, the more coarse the thread.

Threads are in a range of sizes just like yarns. There are natural threads in Cotton, Linen, Bamboo, Soy, Silk. There are ,also, synthetic threads, such as lurex, blending filaments.

My Crochet Tips about Thread Crochet:

336 Crochet Tips !
The Solutions Book for Crocheters

Laundry Care

Chapter 14

336 Crochet Tips !
The Solutions Book for Crocheters

TIP #129
When you present someone with a fine crocheted garment or item, be sure to write them a note on how to care for the garment.

TIP #130
If possible, include a yarn label; however take the time to write out all the laundry symbols as the recipient may not know how to interpret the symbols properly and my launder the item or garment incorrectly.

After all, you have spent many hours working on the project and therefore would like the recipient to enjoy your creation as much as you did while working on it.

There's no way around it. Stains happen. When they do, just follow these simple guidelines to remove stains.

- Treat stains promptly. A piece of ice is the best when in public and cannot get to a stain remover. Place the ice on the crochet fabric and rub the ice into the fabric. Get a white napkin or paper towel and press on the stain to pull some of the stain from the fabric. You may have to repeat this process more than one time.
- Fresh stains are easier to remove than old ones. If the stain is on a non-washable crochet fabric, take it to the dry cleaner as soon as possible. Tell them what kind of substance the stain is (wine, spaghetti sauce, blood, etc) and the fiber content of the crochet garment.
- 3% Hydrogen Peroxide is a good stain remover and can be purchased from your local pharmacy. It is especially effective on wine, spaghetti sauce, blood, and ink.

Dry Cleaning Symbols

⊠ Do not dry clean

Ⓐ Dry cleanable in all solvents

Ⓕ Dry cleanable with fluorocarbon or petroleum-based solvents only

Ⓟ Dry cleanable with perchlorethylene, hydrocarbons, or a petroleum-based solvent

Pressing

⊠ Do not iron

Cool iron

Warm iron

Hot iron

Washing

⊠ Do not wash

Hand wash in warm water

Hand wash at stated temperature

Machine wash

⊠ Do not tumble dry

Tumble drying OK

Dry flat

⊠ No bleach

Chlorine bleach OK

336 Crochet Tips !
The Solutions Book for Crocheters

Adding Yarn &
Basic Color Changes

Chapter 15

TIP # 131
There comes a time when all good things must come to an end.

Yarn is no exception—there is only so much yarn in a skein, a hank, or a ball. Just because the yarn comes to an end, does not mean the project has come to an end.

TIP # 132

Basic Color changes
and Adding A Color

Reminder: Methods for changing to a different yarn color and adding more yarn of the same color are   both part of the same initial process.

{NOTE: Colorwork crochet is an advance process, and is not addressed here in the Basics.}

Tips # 133 – 140

How to Add Yarn at the Beginning or End of A Row

Method 1--Tying a knot method:
Tip # 133
⌘ **Easiest method to add yarn is at the** *end of the row;* **or add yarn at the** *beginning of a row*.

Tip # 134
⌘ **The best knot is simply called the "Surgeon's knot":** Twist the two yarns around each other 3 times about 3 inches from the ends.   Take both ends of the yarn and twist ends around each other 5 times. **Gently, pull on evenly on the 4 strands until the knot tightens onto itself.**

Tip #135
⌘   **Weave the two left over strands into the base of the stitches. Weave the yarns up to the top of the stitches, then pick up the Back Loop on the top stitch and weave the ends around a series of back loops on the top stitches.**

Tip # 136
⌘ Or you can make a simple "Overhand knot" and weave the loose ends into the base of stitches. **NOTE: this will leave telltale sign of where you changed yarns.**

Tip # 137
⌘ **Always tighten the knot by individually tugging on the old strand or color, then new strand or color.**

Tip # 138

⌘ Tie a knot to join the two pieces of yarn together **approximately 6- to 8- inches from the edge.** Because crochet is a "looping" lace, the loops may work their way right back out of the project if you work right up to the end of the yarn.

Tip #139

⌘ *CAUTION!* tying a knot may create odd shaped holes and spaces in the crochet fabric.

Tip # 140

After the knot is tied at the beginning or end of the row, chain the appropriate number and continue crocheting with the new color or new skein of yarn.

TIP #141
Number of chains to turn at the beginning of row:

Ch-1 to turn on a single crochet	X = 1 ◯ to turn.
Ch-2 to turn on a half double crochet	T = 2 ◯◯ to turn.
Ch-3 to turn on a double crochet	= 3 ◯◯◯ to turn.
Ch-4 to turn on a triple crochet	= 4 ◯◯◯◯ to turn.

Crochet symbols in this section provided by Knitware
^{tm}, British Columbia, Canada as a crochet symbols font.

TIP # 142
Method 2—Weaving yarn ends in

⌘ Try to conceal the ends by working the next few stitches over them, or weave the ends at a later time as part of the finishing process.

⌘ **The long ends of waste yarn can be worked into the seams or woven back into the project.**

Tip #143
Changing Yarn in the Middle of the Row:

⌘ **Method 1:** Purchase a small binder clip from an office supply store

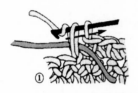

⌘ Cut the old color approximately 6- to 8- inches. Starting 6- to 8- inches from the new yarn's end, **attach the new yarn with the small binder-clip, about 3 to 4 inches back onto the current row's part of the row you have already worked.** This holds the new yarn in place. Continue to work your crochet in the

established pattern.

Tip # 144

⌘ **Method 2:** hold the end of the new yarn along the top working row before finishing off the old yarn; and then work the stitches over it.

⌘ You will see two extra strands hanging at this point: One is the old yarn; and one is the new yarn. Continue crocheting.

Tip # 145

Method 3: Primarily used for double crochet. To join a new yarn or another color in the middle of the row, work the last stitch using the old ball or color, up to the point where the last 2 loops are remaining loops on the hook. Position the old color so that you can crochet on it. To add the new color, I always use a small binder clip and clip the new yarn a few stitches to the right side of where the change will take place. Then, complete the double crochet stitch with the new yarn .

TIP # 146

⌘ **For example, when adding yarn or changing colors while working a dc, work the following: YO, into the stitch with the old yarn, YO, pull through 2 loops; see 2 loops on the hook.   Drop the old yarn. Pick up the new yarn and YO   to complete the stitch in the new yarn.**

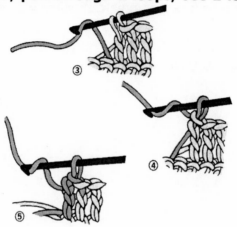

TIP # 147

⌘ Don't   worry about   trying to weave the two yarns at this point, just keep going with the project.

TIP # 148

⌘ **Recommendation:**   Weave all yarn ends as part of the finishing process.

TIP # 149

⌘ Depending upon how long a piece of yarn you have hanging, you can then crochet this yarn right back into the project as you work.

Tip # 150

⌘ **Method 4:**

(This method works best for same color yarns) Unwind 6- to 8- inches of the new yarn. Take a smaller crochet hook Size C or D (2.75mm or 3.25mm), then weave the loose yarn around the back loop (BL) several stitches back, Yarn Over (YO) and pull the new yarn through the stitch. Repeat this process for about five or six stitches.

⌘ **Continue to crochet** in pattern stitch with the new yarn.

⌘ Don't worry about trying to weave the two yarns at this point, just keep going with the project.

⌘ **Recommendation:**   Weave all yarn ends as part of the finishing process.

TIP # 151
Reminders and Recommendations for Adding Yarn and Basic Color Changes

1. ***Create reasons*** to add yarns or change colors. The more you practice these methods, the easier they become. Practice! Practice! *Practice Adding yarns and changing colors.*

2. Allow all the yarn ends to collect throughout the project and *weave them all in at the end of the project.*   In this way, you do not have to stop the crocheting process.

3. If you have changed a lot of colors and knotted the two new yarns together, this may become a *design feature.* Pull all the ends to the public side of the garment, and add beads to the waste yarn ends.

4. When several colors are being used, you will need to *work with separate balls of yarn or bobbins* to keep each color separate.

5. If there are many color changes, the designer usually provides a graphed chart.   Odd rows will begin on the lower right and even rows will begin on the left. *Photocopy the chart onto a transparency and flip it over at the end of each row.*   In this way you always have the current row either on your right (right-hand crochet) or on your left (left-hand crochet).

6. Mosaic type crochet can be used with different colors by using the elongated single crochet. *Instead of working in the current row below, drop down 2 rows or 3 rows below and work the sc.* This will create an unusual pattern in a different color.

Gauge Basics

Chapter 16

336 Crochet Tips !
The Solutions Book for Crocheters

TIP # 152

Gauge is the formula to help you crochet from a published commercial pattern, or create your own pattern from any crochet stitch dictionary pattern.

TIP # 153

⌘   First, **Crochet a practice sample swatch** using the specified hook and yarn if you can find it

⌘   If not, see Chapter 10 on "**Yarn Basics**" to find a comparable yarn.

TIP # 154

⌘   Work the number of stitches and rows to measure a 4" or 10 cm square.

⌘   Place the sample on a flat surface.

TIP #155

⌘   Try not to stretch the sample as you measure the center $2''^{1}$ both horizontally and vertically.

TIP #156

⌘   [NOTE: Purchase a Quilter's Square to assist with accuracy in counting stitches.   You can find the quilter's square in your local craft store in the quilting section.   I use a 9 ½ by 9 ½ inch quilters square to help me obtain accurate gauge.]

Tip # 157

⌘   Mark the stitch positions with vertical pins.

TIP #158

⌘   Mark the row positions with horizontal pins.

TIP #159

⌘   Two-inch increments is usually the smallest "group" of stitches or rows used as a guide in a commercial pattern. This is because the average crochet stitch pattern will repeat itself within a 2-inch distance across the row.

TIP # 160

⌘   If the finished project measurement is divisible by 3", then make the smallest gauge measurement based on number of stitches in 3 inches. If the finished project measurement is divisible by 4", then make the smallest gauge measurement based on (fill in the blank) ____ number of stitches in 4 inches. For example, if you use 4" as the center, then you want to crochet the swatch at least 5" or 6" wide to get an accurate number.

TIP # 161

Recommendation: *Use whatever size hook will give you the correct gauge regardless of the size specified in the pattern!*

You may have to try many different hook sizes and change the yarn a few times.

This is what is meant by "Check Gauge" in a commercial pattern.

TIP # 162

Stitches = horizontal measurement
COUNTING YOUR STITCHES IS IMPORTANT !

Rows = Vertical measurement
COUNTING YOUR ROWS IS IMPORTANT !

TIP # 163

Stitches and rows rely on a conversion
to/from inches or centimeters.

TIP #164

⌘   After about 2 inches when worked in yarn, and approximately 3 inches when worked in thread, **Count the number of stitches in a two-inch section** in the center of the gauge swatch. Be sure to include chain stitches as part of the count especially if they are part of the stitch pattern. For example, place pins on both sides of the **2-inch section**; in this section there are, for example, **12 stitches. (Interchange this number for the number of stitches in your pattern).**

TIP # 165

Divide the desired finished measurement of, for example, 42" by 2" (which is the center section measured to find the number of stitches within 2 inches).

TIP # 166

Here is a formula to keep in mind:
For Example:
 42" (the finished bust measurement, substitute your measurement)   ÷ 2" = 21 groups of 2-inch measurements.

TIP # 167

The conversion from inches to stitches is: 21 groups of 12 stitches per group..

Next, **Multiply 12 stitches by the 21 groups = 252 stitches in 42"**

> **For Example: 12 x 21 = 252 stitches in 42 inches.**

Add 4 stitches if you desire a selvage edge to finish your crochet. That is 2 extra stitches on the left-side edge and 2 extra stitches on the right-side edge. (Recommendation: 42" should include ease, which an allowance of extra measurement for comfort).

TIP # 168

Row Gauge

Count the number of rows in a two-inch[2] section in the center of the gauge swatch. Mark this 2-inch section with pins. The lower pin should be at the base of the stitch; the upper pin should be at the top of the stitch.

For example, there are 5 rows in 2 vertical inches.   The desired length is 18 inches from the base to the top of the item.

Divide 18" by 2" = 9. There are 9 groups of 5 vertical rows. 9 x 5 = 45 rows from beginning to end of item.

Row gauge can be adjusted easier than stitch gauge: Add rows to make the item longer; Or, subtract rows to make the item shorter.

---

[2] **Recommendations for smallest gauge measurement:** If the finished project is divisible by 3" (make the smallest gauge measurement based on number of stitches in 3 inches).   If the finished project is divisible by 4" (make the smallest gauge measurement based on number of stitches in 4 inches).

TIP # 169

If the item is a garment, be sure to try the garment on after you have crocheted approximately 5 to 7 inches.

MY OWN CROCHET TIPS ABOUT GAUGE
MY SOLUTIONS

MY OWN CROCHET TIPS ABOUT GAUGE
MY SOLUTIONS

336 Crochet Tips !
The Solutions Book for Crocheters

Adding stitches
=
Increasing

Chapter 17

Examples of Basic Increases:

TIP # 170

⌘ An increase means that you will work 2 or more times, depending upon the instructions, into the same stitch. In other words, you will be adding stitches to rows in a controlled pattern format.

TIP # 171

⌘ Increases will cause the finished crochet item to become wider at the top of row or the completed item.

TIP # 172

⌘ Some increases will create an unusual stitch texture pattern, which will not increase the sides of the crochet item.   For example, the Shell stitch pattern is based on working 3 or more dc stitches into 1 stitch.

TIP # 173

⌘ In   Filet Crochet **or** To change the shape of a project by increasing, several stitches can be added at the beginning of a row, or at the end of a row. **(See Chart)**

Tɪᴘ # 174

Stitch Increases within a row:		What you will see in the instructions
Sc inc	⋎	**"Sc into same st".** *This means you will work into the stitch a total of two times.*
2 sc inc	⋎	**"Sc into same st 2 more times".** *This means you will work into the same stitch a total of 3 times.*
Hdc inc	V	**"hdc into same st".** *This means you will work into the stitch a total of two times.*
2 hdc inc	V	**"hdc into same st 2 more times."** *This means you will work into the same stitch a total of 3 times.*
Dc inc	V	**"dc into the same st."** *This means you will work into the stitch a total of two times.*
2 dc inc	V	**"dc into the same st 2 more times".** *This means you will work into the same stitch a total of 3 times.*
Shell Stitch	🌟	**"work shell pattern"** . *This means that you will work 5 dc into the same stitch. The shell pattern is a form of increases.*
Open shell stitch	🌟	**" work 2 dc, ch 1, 2 dc into the same stitch".** *This means that you will work 2 dc into the same stitch; then ch 1 stitch,*

Stitch Increases within a row:		What you will see in the instructions
		then work 2 more dc into the same st.
Tr or trc inc	V	"**work 2 tr or trc in same st**". *This means to work 2 trc into the same stitch..*
2 tr or trc inc	V	"**work 3 tr or trc into same st**". *This means you will work into the same stitch a total of 3 times.*

Stitch Increases within a row:		What you will see in the instructions
	Special Increase Stitches	
Popcorn	(symbol)	"Work 5 dc into same st. Pull up a loop and remove hook . Insert hook back into the first dc st; then slide the working loop back onto the hook and pull through the first st. Then ch 1 to lock popcorn." *When working a popcorn stitch pattern, each dc is worked as an individual stitch and then the first dc and the last dc are joined with sl st, then locked with a ch st.*
3-stitch popcorn	(symbol)	"Work 3 dc into same st. Pull up a loop and remove hook . Insert hook back into the first dc st; then slide the working loop back onto the hook and pull through the first st. Then ch 1 to lock popcorn." *When working a popcorn stitch pattern, each dc is worked as an individual stitch and then the first dc and the last dc are joined with sl st, then locked with a ch st.*

These special stitches will have more than one stitch in the process of working them; however the many stitches are classed as one "Popcorn".

Tip # 175

How to add Stitches at the Beginning of a Row

There are several ways to add stitches at the beginning of a row:

⌘ You can increase 1 stitch at the beginning of a row.   For example: In a pattern you may see the following instructions: "Ch 3 turn.   Work 2 dc into 1st dc.   Work dc across row".   The example listed below is in the international format.

➔Row 2

←Row 1

Tip # 176

⌘ **Reminder:**   You read an international symbol in the same direction as you crochet it.   Right-hand crocheters will always crochet to her left on a row pattern; or counterclockwise in a motif round pattern.

Tip # 177

⌘ **Left hand crocheters will always crochet to her right in a row pattern;** or clockwise in a motif round pattern. *Reminder: International crochet symbol patterns are written with right-hand crocheters in mind.*

Tip #178

⌘ **Reminder:** However, left hand crocheters are encouraged to photocopy the international symbols onto a transparency then flip it over and the pattern will be in the best format left-handers.

Tip # 179

⌘ Another method to add stitches at the beginning of a row: Cut 10 to 12 inches of yarn. Make a slip knot and Ch the number of stitches you wish to create.   For example: Ch 5 stitches. Weave in the new yarn at the beginning of the row.   Pick up new row according to instructions.   When you return,   continue in pattern across the 5 new ch stitches.   Weave in ends.   This method keeps the continuity of the stitch pattern or color pattern.

TIP # 180

✻ **You can add several stitches to the beginning of a row to change the shape. You will primarily use this format in Filet Crochet; however you can use it any time you want to increase several stitches at the beginning of a row:**

TIP # 181

How to Add Several Stitches to beginning of a Filet Crochet Row:

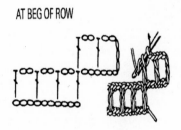

AT BEG OF ROW

Written instructions may read: On **Row 2:** "Work dc into last stitch on foundation ch row.   Ch 11. Turn work.   Work dc into 9th ch from hook. Ch 2, skip 2 ch-sts. Dc into first dc.   Contin in pattern." This method is primarily used to change the shape in a filet crochet item.   This is an "Open Mesh" or "Open Block:" pattern.   You have added 2 extra "Meshes" or "Blocks." **Recommendation: Practice this method before working it into actual project.**

Graphic from: *Magic Crochet Magazine*

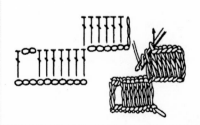

Written instructions may read: On **Row 2:** "Work dc into last stitch on foundation ch row.   Ch 9.   Turn work.   Work dc into 5th ch from hook. Work dc into the next 4 ch-sts. Dc into first dc.   Continue in pattern." This method is primarily used to change the shape in a filet crochet item.   This is a "Solid Mesh or Block " pattern.   You have added 2 extra "Blocks". **Recommendation: Practice this method before working it into actual project.**

Graphic from: *Magic Crochet Magazine*

Tip # 182

How to Add Several Stitches When Starting from a point or a Motif Row:

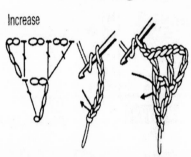

Increase

An increase can be made from a "point".   You will use this method, when you would like to create "diamond"- shape motifs in rows.   You can also use this method   for Filet Crochet.

Instructions may read: "**Row 1**: Ch 6. Work dc into 6th ch from the hook. Ch 5, turn.

Row 2:   Work dc into first dc.   Ch 2, skip 2 sts, into top of 3rd ch work: dc,   ch 2, dc. "   **Note: You are increasing at the beginning and at the end of the row to create the "diamond" pattern".**

Graphic from: *Magic Crochet Magazine.*

Tip # 183
How to add Stitches at the End of a Row

There are several ways to add stitches at the end of a row.   The technique you use to add stitches, sometimes, depends on the overall purpose of the item.

Tip #183

⌘ Some crocheters are natural "increasers" and therefore, they naturally add stitches at the end of row until they learn how to count stitches or "see" the last stitch.

Tip #184

⌘ You can increase 1 stitch at the end of a row. For example: In a pattern you may see the following instructions: "Ch 3 turn. Work dc into 1st dc. Work dc across row. Work 2dc into last st". The example listed below is in the international format.

→**Row 2:**

OOOOOOOOOOOOOOOOOOO **←Row 1**

There may be times when you have to add several stitches at the end of the row.

⌘ See Notes and Reminders above from "How to Add Stitches at the Beginning of a Row".

Tip # 185

⌘ See Tip 179. The difference is that instead of adding stitches at the beginning of the row, you can use the same method to add stitches at the end of the row. Here is how: cut 10 to 12 inches.   Weave in yarn several stitches from the end to use as an anchor.   When you get to the end of the row, make your chain stitches, then turn work and work double crochet or whatever stitch, into the chain stitches. Continue across new row as the pattern indicates.

Tip # 186

⌘ You can add several stitches to the end of a row to change the shape.   You will primarily use this format in Filet Crochet;

however you can use it any time you want to increase several stitches at the end of a row.

TIP #187

How to Add Several Stitches at the end of a Filet Crochet Row:

When several stitches are created at the end of a row, an extended triple stitch or an extended double trc stitch is used to create those last stitches.   Here is how the instructions may be written: End of Row 2... "Work dc into top last dc,   *Ch 2, YO 3 times, work dtr into base of last st worked *.   Repeat from * to * according to instructions."   The graphic here indicates that 2 "open meshes" or "open blocks" have been created.

AT END OF ROW

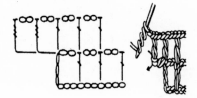

TIP # 188
Recommendation: Practice this method before working it into actual project.

Graphic from *Decorative Crochet Magazine.*

TIP # 189

When several stitches are created at the end of a row where there are no meshes or spaces, an extended double triple stitch or an extended triple trc stitch is used to create the last sts.   Here is how the instructions **may be** written: "Row 2...: Work dc into top last dc, *Ch 2, YO 2 times, work ex tr into base of the last st worked*.   Repeat from * to * according to instructions."   The graphic here indicates that 6 new ex trc sts have been created.
Recommendation: Practice this method before working it into actual project .

Graphic from *Decorative Crochet Magazine*.

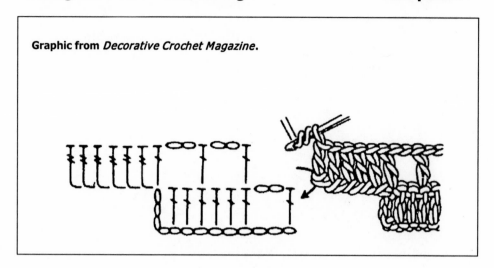

TIP # 190
How to work the Double Treble & the Triple Treble

See Chart on next page:

Double Treble Crochet (dtr)

Step 1: Yo (3 times), insert hook in sixth ch from hook.

Step 2: Yo, draw yarn through st, • yo, draw yarn through 2 loops on hook •, rep from • to • 3 times (1 dtr).

Step 3: Yo (3 times), insert hook in next st, rep from Step 2 for required number of sts.

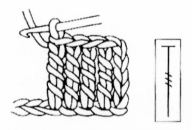

Treble Treble Crochet (trtr)

Step 1: Yo (4 times), insert hook in seventh ch from hook.

Step 2: Yo, draw yarn through st, • yo, draw yarn through 2 loops on hook •, rep from • to • 4 times (1 trtr).

Step 3: Yo (4 times), insert hook in next st, rep from Step 2 for required number of sts.

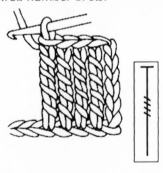

Graphic from Crochet Fantasy Magazine—Published by All American Crafts

TIP # 191
Always practice and try out a newly learned skill.

Tropical Rose Pattern
Rated Easy

Yarn:
- **Class 3 or 4 Yarn, 2 oz. (approximately 40 yards)**

Hook: Appropriate to yarn (check the yarn label) for a recommended size. (Note you can choose to work with one size smaller to make a more compact rose.

Notions:
- **Big eye needle**
- **Scissors**

Stitches used:

Ch	**=**	**Chain stitch**
Sc	**=**	**Single Crochet Stitch**
Dc	**=**	**Double Crochet Stitch**
Trc	**=**	**Triple Crochet Stitch**

Gauge:
Measure row 1: 15 inches.

Finished Gauge:
4 inches after the rose is rolled.

Foundation Rows:
Ch 55.   Turn work to the bumpy side of the ch.
Sc in ea bump across row.   Total 54 sc.   Ch 6, turn work.

Row 1:
Work dc into 1st sc. *Ch 2, sk next 2 sts, in the next sc, work (dc, ch 2, dc).*   Rep from * to * across row.   Total 38 sps.   Turn ch 1.

Row 2:
Sc into 1st ch-2 sp, ch 2.   Work 5 dc in same space (first petal made).   Sc in next ch-2 sp. (6 dc in next ch-2 sp, sc in next ch-2 sp), 4 more times.   Work (9 dc in next ch-2 sp, sc in next ch-2 sp), 5 more times. Work (12 dc in next ch-2 sp, sc in next ch-2), 5 more times or until row is completed. (NOTE OPTION: can work last group of 12 stitches in Trc crochet. This makes the petal larger.)

End off, leave approximately 12 inches of yarn for weaving and sewing.   Roll the Rose, then thread needle with yarn end.   Sew through Row 1 as necessary to keep rose secure.   Best method is to sew in a criss-cross method.

TIP # 192

Some uses of the Tropical Rose:
- Add some artificial rose leaves; stems, and Baby's Breath dried flowers, purchased from your craft store.   Put the rose on the stem and have long stemmed roses in a bud vase.
- Add a brooch pin to the back and wear as an accessory.
- Add a blank hair barrette, add some beads and streamers and have glitzy hair ornament.
- Add gold ribbon and place as a decoration on a wrapped package.

Yarn by *Naturally Caron "Country"*

336 Crochet Tips !
The Solutions Book for Crocheters

Decreasing
=
Subtracting Stitches

Chapter 18

336 Crochet Tips !
The Solutions Book for Crocheters

TIPS # 197 -#199
Examples of Basic Decreases

⌘ A decrease is a form of subtracting stitches from a row or area of a project. For example, when you work a decrease, the pattern will have one or two less stitches on a given row—If the row has 27 stitches; and 1 decrease is worked, then the row will end up with 26 stitches.

⌘ These controlled decreases, will create patterns and textures within the crochet as well as reducing stitches to control shaping of a project

⌘ A decrease is working two stitches together; OR skipping one or more stitches.

TIP # 200 & TIP 201
There are 2 basic methods to decrease:

1. Skip a stitch. This method is good for single crochet or half double crochet.   Recommendation: Do not use this method for dc or trc. It will leave large unsightly holes into the fabric.   These holes can be gaudy unless they are worked as a lace stitch pattern.

2. St2tog, this is a type of "invisible" decrease, because it is difficult to, sometimes, see where it is in the row.   For example dc2tog is worked as follows: YO, insert hook into next st; yo pull thru 2 loops.   2 loops are still on hook; YO, insert hook into next stitch, YO and pull thru, see 4 loops on hook.   YO and pull thru 2 loops, see 3 loops on hook.   YO and pull thru all 3 loops in one motion.   NOTE: this method can be used to "sc2tog"; "hdc2tog"; "trc2tog"

TIP # 202

The process of decreasing, will subtract stitches from a row. Some crocheters avoid patterns, which contain decreases; however with the chart listed below, perhaps the mystery of decreases will be solved.

TIP # 203

Skipping the next stitch, without adding a supporting chain stitch, is a form of decreasing.

Stitches		You may see these instructions
Sc dec or Sc2tog ...	⋏	"Skip the next st. Work sc into next st." *This type of decrease will create a large hole or space in the ...* crochet item. *At times, this can be very gaudy and unsightly..* OR,
Sc dec or Sc2tog	⋏	"Insert hook in next st, YO, pull through 1 loop. See 2 loops on hook. Insert hook in the next stitch and draw up another loop. See 3 loops on hook, YO, and pull through all 3 loops in one motion. Sc dec made." *In this type of decrease, 2 stitches are worked into 1 st; however, using half of 2 sc stitches.*

TIP # 204
REMINDER—The following 8 types of decrease stitches WILL NOT not skip the next stitch.

Stitches		You may see These instructions
3 sc dec OR sc3tog		"Insert hook in next st, YO, pull through 1 loop. See 2 loops on hook. Insert hook in the next stitch and draw up another loop. See 3 loops on hook, YO, and pull through all 1 loop. See 3 loops on hook, YO, pull through 3 loops in one motion. 3-Sc dec made." *In this type of decrease, 3 stitches are worked into 1 st; however, using half of 3 sc stitches.*
Hdc dec OR		"YO, insert hook into the next st, YO pull through. See 3 loops on hook. YO, pull through 1 loop. See 3 loops on hk. YO, Insert hk into next st. YO pull through, see 5 loops on hk. YO, pull through 2 loops. See 4 loops on hk. YO pull through all 4 loops in one motion. Hdc dec made." *In this type of decrease, 2*

Decreasing = Subtracting Stitches   Chapter 18

hdc2tog ...	𝍖	*stitches are worked into 1 st; however, using half of 2 hdc stitches.*
3 hdc dec **OR** **Hdc3tog**	𝍖 𝍖	**"YO, insert hook into the next st, YO pull through. YO, pull through 1 loop. See 3 loops on hook. YO, Insert hook in the next stitch, YO, pull through. See 5 loops on the hook. YO, pull through 2 loops. See 4 loops on hk. YO, insert hook into next stitch YO pull through . See 6 loops on hk. YO pull through 2 loops, YO pull through 5 loops in one motion. 3 Hdc dec made."** *In this type of decrease, 3 stitches are worked into 1 st; however, using half of 3 hdc stitches.*
Dc dec **OR** **Dc2tog...**	𝍖 𝍖	**"YO, insert hook into the next st, YO, pull through; YO pull through 2 loops. See 2 loops on hook. YO, insert hook in the next st, YO, pull through. See 4 loops on the hook ..YO, pull through 2 loops. YO, pull through 3 loops in one motion. Dc dec made."** *In this type of decrease, 2 stitches are worked into 1 st; however, using half of 2 dc stitches.*

336 Crochet Tips !
The Solutions Book for Crocheters

3 dc dec **OR** **dc3tog**	 	"YO, insert hook into the next st, YO, pull through. See 3 loops on hk. YO, pull through 2 loops. YO, Insert hook in the next st, YO, pull through. See 4 loops on the hook. YO, pull through 2 loops. YO, insert hook into the next st, YO, pull through. See 5 loops on hook. YO pull through 2 loops; YO pull through all 4 loops in one motion." *In this type of decrease, 3 stitches are worked into 1 st; however, using half of 3 dc stitches.*
4 dc dec		"YO, insert hook into the next st, YO, pull through. See 3 loops on hk. YO, pull through 2 loops. YO, Insert hook in the next st, YO, pull through. See 4 loops on the hook. YO, pull through 2 loops. Insert hook in the next st, YO, pull through, YO pull through 2 loops . YO Insert hook in the next st, YO, pull through 2 loops, YO pull ... ... through 5 loops in one motion." *In this type of decrease, 4 stitches are worked into 1 st; however, using half of 4 dc stitches.*

OR **dc4tog...**		
Trc dec **OR** **tr2tog**		"YO 2 times. Insert hook into the next st, YO, pull through. [YO pull through 2 loops] 2 times. YO 2 times. Insert hook into the next st, YO, pull through. [YO pull through 2 loops] 2 times. YO pull through all 3 loops in one motion." *In this type of decrease, 2 stitches are worked into 1 st; however, using half of 2 trc stitches.*
3 trc dec **OR** **tr3tog**		"YO 2 times. Insert hook into the next st, YO, pull through. [YO pull through 2 loops] 2 times. YO 2 times. Insert hook into the next st, YO, pull through. [YO pull through 2 loops] 2 times. YO 2 times. Insert hook into the next st, YO, pull through. [YO pull through 2 loops] 2 times. See 4 loops on hook. YO pull through all 4 loops in one motion." *In this type of decrease, 3 stitches are worked into 1 st; however, using half of 3 trc stitches.*

Crochet symbols provided by Janet Tombu, British Columbia, Canada as a Crochet Symbols True Type font.

TIP # 205
& How to Decrease Stitches at the Beginning of a Row.

There are several ways to subtract or decrease stitches at the beginning of a row :

⌘ You can skip 1 stitch at the beginning of a row.

TIP # 206

⌘ In a pattern you may see the following instructions: "Ch 3 turn. Dc into 1st dc. Work Dc2tog in .2 sts. Work dc across row". The example listed below is in the international format.

➜Row 2   (crochet chart diagram)   Row 2

Row 1 ←

chain sts

TIP # 207

⌘ **Recommendation: Do not work dec sts on the very edge of crochet work. Always work 1 or 2 stitches before the dec. Reminder:** You read an international symbol in the same direction as you crochet it. Right hand crocheters will always crochet to her left on a row pattern; or counterclockwise in a motif round pattern.

TIP #208

⌘ **Left hand crocheters will always crochet to her right in a row pattern;** or clockwise in a motif round pattern.   *Reminder: International crochet symbol patterns are written with right-hand crocheters in mind.*

TIP #209

⌘ **Reminder:** However, left hand crocheters are encouraged to photocopy the international symbols onto a transparency then flip it over and the pattern will be in the best format left-handers.

TIP #210

⌘ You can decrease several stitches to the beginning of a row to change the shape.   You will primarily use this format in Filet Crochet; however you can use it any time you want to decrease several stitches at the beginning of a row

TIP # 211
How to Decrease Stitches at the Beginning of
a Row Using Slip Stitches

**Arrows
indicate
Direction
of work for
right hand
crocheter:**

AT BEG OF ROW

① work sl sts to dec

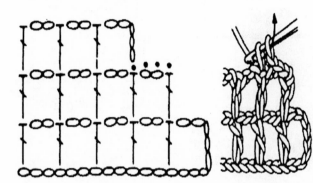

← Row 3

→ Row2

← Row 1

Chains→

This method of decreasing at the beginning of Row 2, after the turn, <u>uses slip stitches</u> to decrease to Row 3 and change the shaping.

Graphics from *Decorative Crochet Magazine*

Instructions may read:

"Ch 21. Row 1: Dc into the 9th ch from hook.   * Ch 2, sk 2 sts, dc in next st. * Repeat from * to * across row. End row with dc in last ch. (see 5 spaces).

Row 2: Ch 3. Dc into 1st dc. *ch 2, sk 2 sts, dc into next st.*   Repeat 3 more times. Ch 1, turn.

 Row 3: sl st into last dc and into next 2 ch-sts. Ch 5. Work dc into 3rd dc. [Ch 2, sk 2 sts, dc into next dc] 1 more time."

Tip # 212
How to Decrease Stitches at the Beginning of a Row Using Long Triple Crochet or TrTrc Stitches

**Arrows
indicate
Direction
of work for
right hand
crocheter:**

 ← Row 3

 → Row2

 ← Row 1
 Chains→

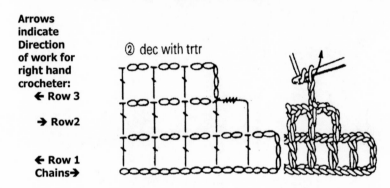

② dec with trtr

Graphics from: Decorative Crochet Magazine

This method of decreasing at the beginning of Row 2, after the turn, <u>uses TrTrc stitches</u> to decrease on Row 3 and change the shaping.

Instructions may read:

"Ch 21. Row 1: Dc into the 9th ch from hook.   * Ch 2, sk 2 sts, dc in next st. * Repeat from * to * across row. End row with dc in last ch. (see 5 spaces).

Row 2: Ch 3. Dc into 1st dc. *ch 2, sk 2 sts, dc into next st.* Repeat 3 more times. *YO, 4 times. In last dc work TrTrc, turn.* Ch 5 turn.

Row 3: Work dc into 2nd dc. [Ch 2, sk 2 sts, dc into next dc] 1 more time."

TIP # 213
How to Decrease stitches At End of Row Using Long Triple Crochet or TrTrc Stitches

Arrows indicate Direction of work for right hand crocheter:

AT END OF ROW

1 trtr with 1 dc

Graphic from:

← Row 3

→ Row2

← Row 1

Chains→

Decorative Crochet Magazine

Instructions may read:

"Row 1... *dc into next st, ch 2*, repeat from * to * to last 3 sts. YO 4 times, work TrTrc into last ch. Ch 5 turn.

Row 2: Sk 2 ch-sts. [dc into next dc, ch 2, sk 2 sts] 1 more time. Dc into last dc.

Row 3: ... dc into next dc, ch 2, sk 2 sts. YO 4 times, In last dc work TrTrc".
This method of decreasing at the end of Row 1, before turning, uses TrTrc stitches to dec Row 1 and change the shaping at the end of the Rows 2 & 3.

TIP # 214
How to Decrease stitches At End of Row Using Long Triple Crochet or TrTrc Stitches

Arrows indicate Direction of work for right hand crocheter:

→ Row2

← Row 1 Chains→

work 4 partial dc, dec with 4-dc cluster

Graphics are from Decorative Crochet Magazine

This method of decreasing at the end of a row is primarily used with filet crochet and to used to change the shape of an item.

Instructions may read:

Row 1: ... *dc into next st, ch 2, sk 2 sts *. Repeat from * to * across row to last 4 stitches.   Work half dc sts as follows: ◊YO, insert hook into   next ch, YO pull thr. YO pull through 2 loops ; ◊ Repeat from ◊ to ◊ 3 more times.   See 5 loops on hook. YO, pull through all 5 loops in one motion. Ch 3, turn
ROW 2: Work 2 dc into ch-2 space. * Dc into next dc, ch 2, sk 2 sts, dc into next*...

TIP # 215
How to Decrease At the Beginning & At the End of the Row

**Arrows
indicate
Direction
of work for
right hand
crocheter:**

➔ **Row2**

⬅ **Row 1**

Chains➔

*On Row 2 Ch-3 and dc = dec; dc2tog at end of row = dec. These 2
dec represent decreases on both side of work to alter shaping.*

Instructions may read:
"Ch 18.

Row 1... Dc in the 9th ch from the hook. Ch 2, sk 2 sts. *Dc into
next ch-st; ch 2, skip 2*. Repeat from * to * across row to last dc.
Row 2... Ch 3, sk the ch-2 space. * Dc into next dc, ch 2, sk 2 sts*.
Repeat from * to * across row to last dc. In last dc, work dc to last
two loops on hook. Do not complete. With 2 loops on hk, YO,
insert hook into 3 ch, YO, complete dc."

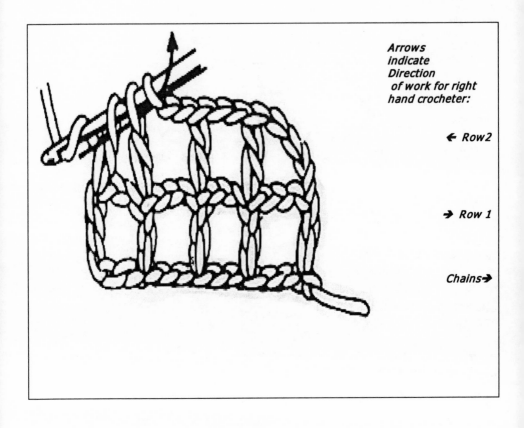

Arrows
indicate
Direction
of work for right
hand crocheter:

← Row2

→ Row 1

Chains→

MY CROCHET TIPS
MY SOLUTIONS

Decreasing = Subtracting Stitches   **Chapter 18**

Motifs:
Working in Rounds

Section 19

TIP # 216

Crochet can be worked in rows, ROUNDS, or a combination of both methods. When crochet is worked in rounds it can formulate motifs in various geometric shapes and sizes, depending upon the number of rounds completed and the number of corners completed. This is basic geometry. Not to worry, I have done the math for you. Listed below are some examples of motifs and the number of corners/sided.

TYPE OF MOTIF	Basic Shapes	Number of corners/sides
TRIANGLE ; OR 3-SIDE STAR OR FLOWER	△ ▲ ✦	3
SQUARE ; (KNOWN AS "GRANNY"	▣ ◈ ▦ ✤ ▢ ✦	4
PENTAGON; OR 5-SIDED FLOWER ; OR STAR	❀ ⬟ ⬟ ★ ✳	5
HEXAGON; OR 6-SIDED FLOWER ; OR STAR	⬣ ⬣ ✳ ✦ ✡	6
OCTAGON ; OR 8-SIDED FLOWER ; OR STAR	⬢ ✳ ✴	8
10-SIDED DOILY OR 12- SIDED	⬢	10 +

DOILY		
CIRCLE OR OVAL	◎ ◯	

TIP # 217
Symbols vs. Words

Some crocheters prefer to work from the international symbols, while other crocheters prefer words. I prefer to work with crochet symbols, because I am a visual person. Perhaps working with the crochet symbol patterns is new to you. Take an adventure and try a new technique.

TIP # 218

⌘ When desiring to make a motif, it is better to follow the international symbol patterns; because they are easier to follow than the word patterns. Adage: picture/graphic is worth a 1000 words.

TIP # 219

⌘ **Recommendation:** When working from symbol charts, **first:** go and look for the number "1". It will always show you where to begin.

TIP # 220

⌘ **THE ASSUMPTION:** The international assumption is that all crocheters are right-handed. While we know this is not true, the patterns are all written based on right-hand crocheters. Therefore, you "read/interpret" the pattern from right to left.

TIP # 221

⌘ **LEFT HAND CROCHETERS:** International symbols are best for left-hand crocheters, because there is a graphic to work from. Left-handers do not have to "convert" word patterns into the directions, which is best for them.
   o Photo copy the pattern onto a transparency

○ Flip the transparency over, and Eureka!, the pattern flows in the direction best for left hand crocheters

TIP # 222

⌘ Once you invest the time to learn the international crochet symbols, you can crochet from any book around the world or interpret the patterns in any language, just by knowing the symbols.   The symbols do not change from language to language (for example, from French to German). So you don't really need a lot of words: primarily a finished photo and the symbol graphic chart.

TIP # 223

⌘ Keep your favorite highlighter in your crochet kit. Photocopy your symbol pattern; then highlight sts as you go.   Even though this seems slow at first, it is an accurate method to keep track of where you are in the pattern.   Once your eyes become accustomed to looking at the symbol charts, you may no longer need to highlight the pattern.

TIP # 224

Here is an example of working in symbols vs. words. 4 Graphics are from the American School of Needlework: _**Learn To Do Symbol Crochet In Just One Day**_ by Jean Leinhauser.

TIP # 225
How to Follow A Symbol Pattern in 4 Basic Steps:

Symbol	Words

TIP # 225 A
RECOMMENDATION: ALWAYS FIND THE #1 IN A SYMBOL PATTERN. THAT IS WHERE YOU ARE TO BEGIN THE CROCHET.

Symbol	Words
	Ch 6, and join with a sl st to form a ring.
Rnd 1:	Rnd 1: ch 4 (counts as a trc), work 23 trc in the ring (not into the chain st); join with sl st in the 4th ch of beg ch-4). Total 24 trc.
Rnd 2:	Rnd 2: Ch 1, sc in same ch-sp as joining; ch 5; *sk next trc, sc, in next trc, ch5; rep from * 10 more times; join with sl st in 1st sc. Total 12 spaces, with ch 5 in each space.

Symbol	Words
Rnd 3: 	**Rnd 3:** Sl st in next 3 chs, ch 1. Sc in same ch as last sl st made; ch 5, [sc in 3rd ch fof next ch-5 spa; then ch 5] 11 times; join in first sc. **NOTE:** When you finish these 4 steps, our crochet should look like the chart.

This Chart provided by Yo's Needlework

Here is how a symbol pattern appears in a publication.

With color A, ch 5, sl st in 1st ch to form a ring.
Rnd 1: Ch 3, work 15 dc in the ring. Sl st in top of the ch-

Symbol	Words

3. Total: 16 dc

Rnd 2: Ch 4. *1 dc in dc of last row, ch1*. Repeat from * to * around. Sl st in 3rd ch of beg ch-4. (Optional: Cut thread, and attach color B)

Rnd 3: Ch 1. *work 3 hdc cluster st in ch-1 sp. Ch 3 *. Repeat from * to * around, ending with sl st in top of 1st cluster st. (Optional: cut thread, and attach Color C in ch-3 sp)

Rnd 4: Ch 1 and sc in same sp under ch. Ch 4, sc in next ch-3 sp, ch 4. *sc in next ch-3 sp, ch4, sc in next ch-3 sp [2 more times]; ch 5*. Repeat from * to * end with ch 2 and hdc in top of beg sc.

Rnd 5: Ch 1, sc on top of hdc. Ch 5, 1 sc in 1st ch-4sp; ch 5; 3 dc, ch 5, 3 dc in next ch-5 sp.* Ch 5. 1 Sc in next ch-4 sp, [2 more times], ch 5, 3 dc, ch 5 , 3 dc in next ch-5 sp for corner*. Repeat from * to * around, ending with sl st in beg sc. Cut thread and finish off.

TIP # 226
Laws of Motifs

The Laws of Motifs—If this sounds serious, it is.   So the question arises, what are the "Laws of Motifs"?   The basic premise is this: You have to follow certain rules, or you will not make the intended motif. Here is an example from my Crochet Basics Class:

TIP # 227

LAW # 1

Motifs begin in the center.   The basic motif begins with "chain 5, and join with a slip stitch to form a ring".

TIP # 228

Here is how to make the "No-Chain Start".   NOTE: this method is also called the "Adjustable Ring Start; "Loop Start"—and knowing you, you will come up with another name for this method.   (See Diagram)

THE NO-CHAIN START METHOD

1. FORM A LOOP AT THE END OF THE YARN:

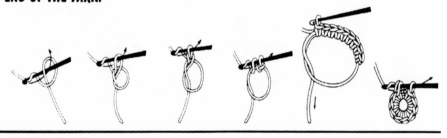

OR,
2. FORM A DOUBLE LOOP AT THE END OF THE YARN.

Graphic from Decorative Crochet Magazine, 2001

TIP # 229

I digress: This method was invented by the Japanese as part of their contributions to International Crochet symbols.   There are times when you do not want to see "hole" in the center of the motif, because some motifs look better WITHOUT the doughnut hole in the center.

Using the motif on the opposite page as an example,   we see how the "Laws of Motif Corners" work.

Note: Pattern #91 is an actual international pattern. The number "1" is on its side; however simply turn the pattern. See Tip #232, this is a close up of center of Pattern #91.

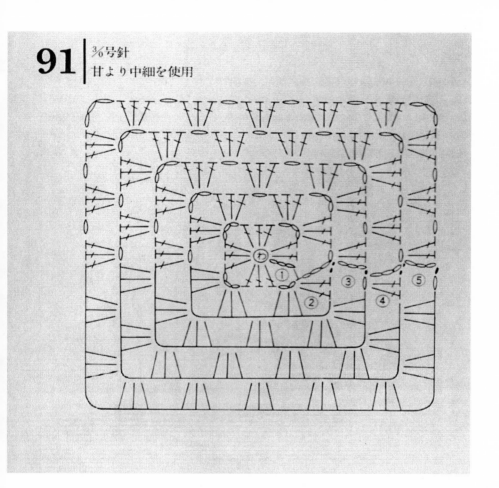

91 | ⅜号針
甘より中細を使用

Tip # 230

You need two crochet "buddies" when learning to read an International crochet pattern: 1) Work with a highlighter to "color" the stitches as you work them. Accuracy is more important than speed; and, 2) place marker on each corner so that your eyes can "see" where the corners are as you go round and round.

TIP # 231

Law # 2: You have to KNOW certain things about motifs.   **LAW OF CORNERS**. A motif does not grow or "increase at the corners". It grows, or increases along the sides.   So, therefore, if you make one mistake on the corner, the whole motif will be affected and will not result in the desire geometric shape**.**   **KNOW**

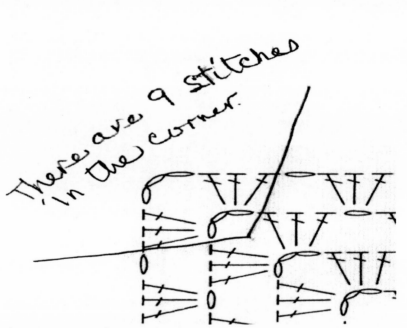

HOW MANY STITCHES ARE IN THE CORNER. In this motif, there are 9 stitches in the corner.

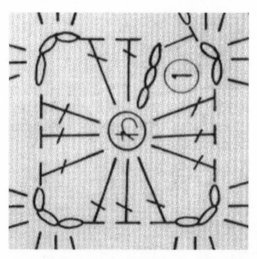

TIP # 232

LAW #3:   Go find the NUMBER 1 in the pattern. This will indicate WHERE YOU WILL BEGIN THE PATTERN. In this pattern, you will begin in the center. Though the (1) is on its side, begin slightly to the left of the (1) with ch 3.

TIP # 233

Use a highlighter to highlight the crochet symbols pattern as you go. In this way, you will keep track of where you are in the pattern.

TIP # 234

LAW #4:   You read the pattern in the direction which you crochet.   For example,   If you are a right-hand crocheter, you will ALWAYS be crocheting to you your LEFT.   So, therefore, you "read" an international crochet pattern to the LEFT of the NUMBER 1 or counterclockwise on a motif.

TIP # 235

LEFT-HAND CROCHETERS: Note: purchase a transparency. Have the pattern copied onto the transparency.   Turn the transparency over.   The pattern will then be on the Left-hand side or clockwise. Left hand crocheters MUST WORK WITH A TRANSPARENCY and then flip it over so that you are "reading" and international pattern in the correct direction for a left-hand crocheter, which is clockwise on a circular motif.

TIP # 236

LAW #5: Understanding *   * (the asterisk or   how to REPEAT A PATTERN IN INTERNATIONAL SYMBOL CROCHET). On the top of the pattern, you can plainly see the stitches. However, if you look to the bottom of the pattern, it appears as   though al the stitches have changed to look similar to the half-double crochet pattern.   This is the *   * or "repeat what you did on top side of the diagram.

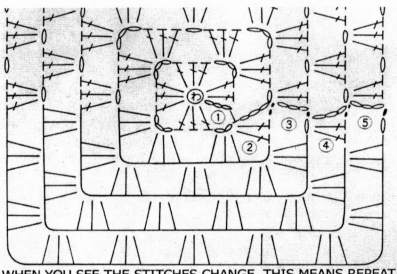

WHEN YOU SEE THE STITCHES CHANGE, THIS MEANS REPEAT WHAT YOU DID ON THE OPPOSITE SIDE OF THE MOTIF.

Please refer to the Chapter 7 on International Crochet Symbol charts for more information.

TIP # 237

Here are several examples of international patterns.   Using the
Crochet Tips is this section, challenge yourself to work at least one
motif.

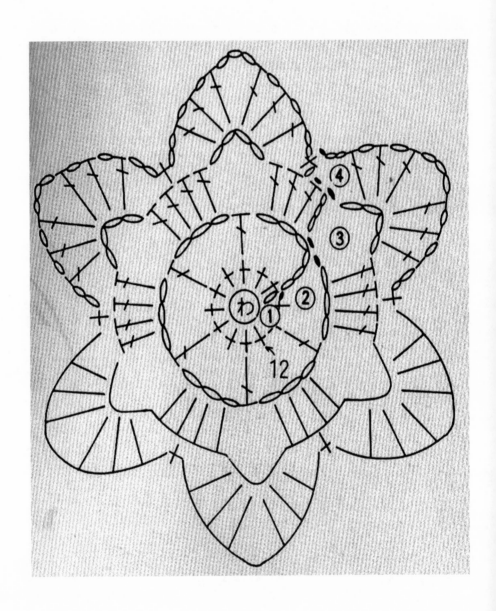

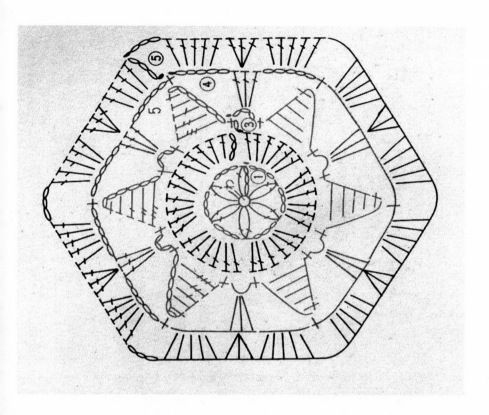

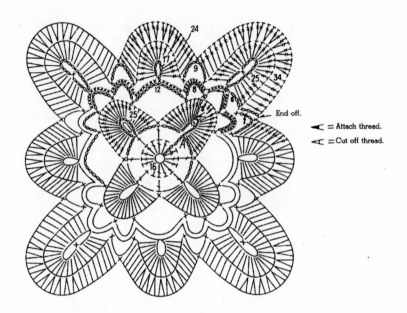

= Attach thread.
= Cut off thread.

Tip # 238

There are several ways to join motifs for a pleasing arrangement. Try to join motifs as you crochet, because the finishing is easier and the motifs look better.

Here are some of the ways that motifs can be joined together:

TIP #239

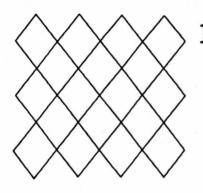 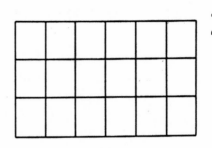

Joining Squares

There are 2 key methods featured above for joining square motifs. Method 1 represents joining motifs at 90 degree angles to form square diamond. Method 2 represents joining squares into rows.

TIP # 240
Joining Hexagons

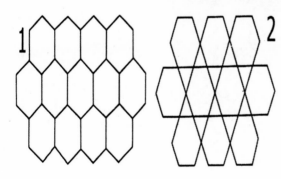 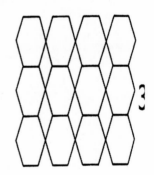

There are 3 methods for joining hexagons. Method 1 is commonly referred to as the honeycomb method, because this is the method that bees use to build a honeycomb. Method 2 is alternating hexagons and small triangles holes form between the hexagons. A second motif can be used in the triangle space. Method 3 hexagons are stacked on top of each other. This creates a diamond space between the hexagon. A simple diamond motif can be worked in the spaces.

TIP # 241
Joining Triangles

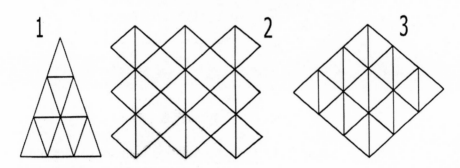

There are 3 methods to join triangles and each method creates a different shape. Method 1 creates a larger triangle; Method 2 creates squares and triangles; and method 3 creates a modified diamond.

TIP # 242

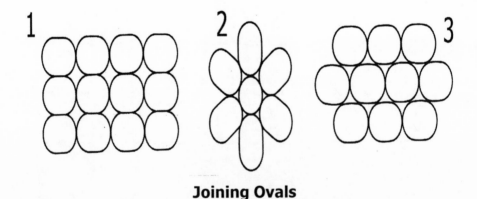

Joining Ovals

There are 3 methods for joining ovals. Note: there will always be spaces between ovals no matter, which method you use to join the oval motif.

TIP # 243
Joining Octagons

There are 3 methods for joining Octagons.

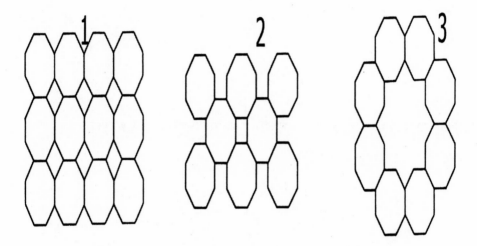

Tip # 244
Joining Circle Motifs

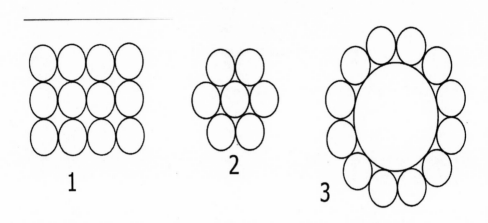

1   2   3

Circle motifs can be joined together in many different ways.

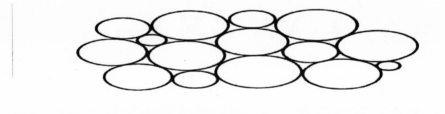

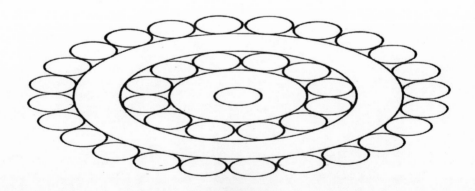

Tᴉᴘ # 245
Joining various motifs

It is possible to join motif with several different shapes.　Here are several methods to join various shapes of motifs together.　You can even use fabric to substitute one of the motifs.

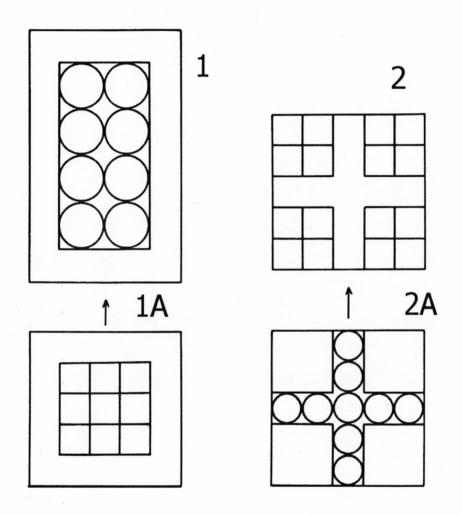

MY CROCHET TIPS !
MY SOLUTIONS

336 Crochet Tips !
The Solutions Book For Crocheters

Basics of
Edgings & Insertions

Chapter 20

---

[1] All graphics in this section are from *Decorative Crochet/Magic Crochet Magazines*

Tip #246
Important !!

Start all edgings either in the middle of the piece or a few inches from the corner.   Do not start an edging at the corner !!   It is harder to fudge if you miscalculated   the number of stitches on the finishing rounds.

Tips # 247 - 254
Edging Basics:

⌘ Edgings are primarily worked last. They are the finishing portion of a motif, a doily, a garment, or an afghan.

- However, anything is possible and you may chose to work the edging first and then attach yarn, and crochet the garment or accessory from the bottom up; therefore the bottom of the garment will be finished when you have finished the top of the garment.

⌘ Some edgings can be worked separate from the item, then joined to the item once the item is finished.

⌘ Edgings fall into 3 categories: Rounded or scalloped sequences; pointed or Van Dyke sequences; and squared or Castled sequences.

⌘ A Rounded or scalloped sequence refers to an edging which forms large scallops or shells on the edge.

⌘ A pointed or Van Dyke sequence refers to an edging which forms large points on the edge.   These points can be made with decreases or cluster stitches.

⌘ A Squared or Castled edging refers to an sequence which forms variations of squares along the edging.

✿ Edgings usually create a very lacy border, which draws the eye back to the middle of the item; the border repeats a sequence of pattern stitches, which have been worked within the motif or doily.

✿ An edging has one straight side, which is usually worked into or attached to the body of the work; and one edge, which is rounded, pointed, or squared. (see above).

TIP # 255
Reminders:
- Any of the edgings featured in this section can be used on any garment, afghan, doily or motif.
- The more lacy the edging, the more the eye will be attracted to follow the edgings pattern.
- Some edgings will look better in thread than in yarn—play with the edging before working onto the item.

TIP # 256
Sample of Scallop Type Edging

✿ **Scallop edgings will mostly have a combination of stitches, which form shell-like patterns.**

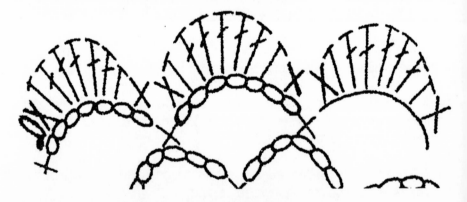

This is a type of scalloped or rounded edging.

✿ Review the "International symbols" in Chapter 7.

TIP # 257

⌘ Beads have to be strung on after the motif or doily is finished; break thread; then string on beads; work round 1 of edging..

TIP # 258

⌘ Picots can be a standard reliable edging for a quick finishing. Picots complement any item and add a touch of elegance no matter the yarn or thread, no matter how dressy or casual the item.

TIP # 259
Sample of Van Dyke Type Edging
Van Dyke Edgings will usually form a pointed edging.

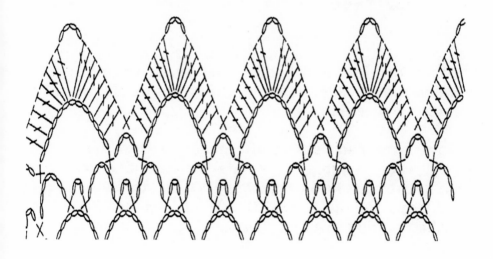

TIP # 260
Example of a Castle-Type Edging
- **Castle-type edgings have a resemblance of ancient castle roof tops**

- Picots are one of the key features included with the castle-type edgings.

- To work a picot (⊕), chain 3, and slip st ● into top of the ⅄

- Review the "International symbols" in Chapter 7.

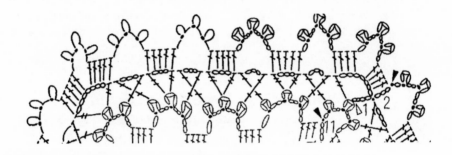

TIP # 261

Example of Picot and beads used as an edging. When working with beads, you can string the beads on before you start the edging.

Use the extended version of stitches to hold the bead in place.   For example, to create the extended dc: Yarn over, insert hook into next stitch, YO, pull through (pl thr), see 3 loops on your hook, YO pl thr 1 loop, see 3 loops on your hook, bring bead up (BBU) YO, pl thr 2 loops, YO, pl thr 2 loops.

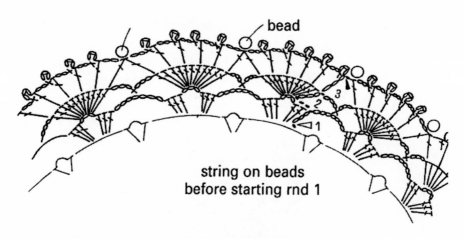

bead

string on beads
before starting rnd 1

TIP # 262
Beading To The Front Side of Crochet

For example, if you are working on a motif and specifically want the bead to stay on the front side of work rather than falling to back and having to use the "back" of item as the "front", here is the method to use.   (Beading to the front can only be worked with stitches, which begin with a Yarn Over (YO).

Examples of stitches, which you can bead to the front are: Hdc, Extended Hdc,   Dc, Extended Dc, Trc and extended Trc.

Here is how to work beading to the front.   Bring bead up (BBU) next to hook, YO.   Work extended dc as follows: Insert hook into next stitch, YO pull thru (pl thr), see 3 loops on your hook. YO pl thr 1 loop, and still see 3 loops on your hook; YO pl thr 2 loops, slide bead, YO pl thr 2 loops, bead will be in the middle of the stitch.

TIP # 263
Shell stitch pattern makes a wonderful edging on a motif

Example of Shell Pattern and Single Crochet as edging on a Motif

This octagon motif uses the shell st pattern and the sc. By using the sc, an insertion of ch sts can be used to join two of these motifs together.

TIP # 264
Example of Shell Stitch Pattern Used as an Edging

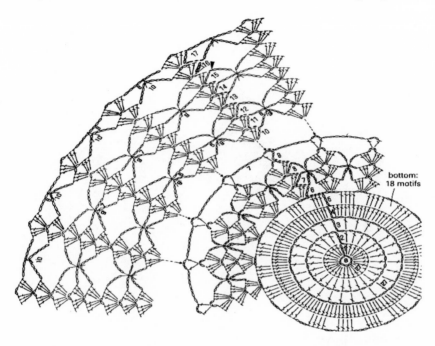

Graphic: Magic/Decorative Crochet Magazine.

Shell st pattern can be used as an edging. This shell pattern st is combined with long lengths of ch sts.

TIP # 265
Best Practices with this edging:

⌘   When using this type of edging, counting the ch sts, accurately, is the key.

⌘   It is the chain sts, which will cause the edging to lay flat and not ripple.

TIP # 266
Chain stitches make a versatile edging

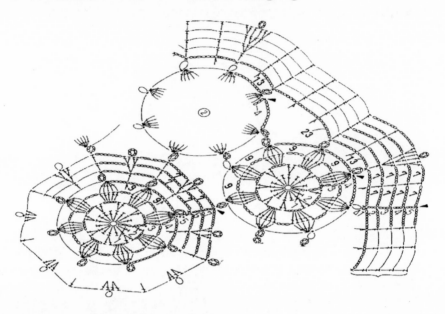

Graphic: Magic/Decorative Crochet Magazine.

Best Practices:
- ⌘ Notice the same motif is worked with rows of extra ch sts and one motif is worked without the extra rows of ch sts.
- ⌘ The edging then is worked in ch sts to carry the central theme to the edge of work, so the eye can find the same pattern within the work.

TIP # 267
Edging worked on a square motif

bead

Best Practices Using this type of Edging:

⌘ The edging of this motif formed into a square based on the last three rows.

⌘ On the 1st round of the edging is the shaping round and basis for the square.

⌘ 2nd round increased the shell pattern from "2 ⋎, ○ 3, 2 ⋎" and increased to "3 ⋎, ○ 3, 3 ⋎."

TIP # 268
Edgings can be used to Frame Groups of Small Motifs

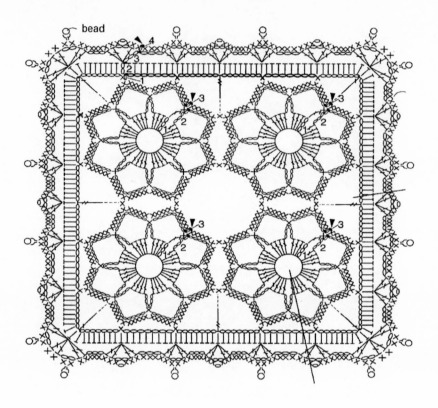

Best Practices Using this type of Edging:

- ⌘ When you frame small motifs as an edging, counting the connecting stitches is vital to the success of the edging.
- ⌘ For example, Round 1 of this edging is based on ch stitches. Notice there are more stitches in the corners than along the side edges.
- ⌘ Edging on Round 1-- Ch Stitches are used as the foundation for this edging
- ⌘ Round 2, Hdc stitches are the basis of the stability in this edging.
- ⌘ Round 3, the shell pattern adds a laciness to the pattern.
- ⌘ **Reminder:** On Round 3 the corner shell stitch pattern, have more stitches than along the sides. This is to assist the frame to **lay flat.**

TIP # 269
Small Motifs can be crocheted as an edging:

Best Practices for this type of edging:
- ⌘ When small motifs are used as an edging, it is best that the small motifs **(A)** are joined as you work.
- ⌘ For Example, the center **(B)** motifs are worked first.   As the center small motif is worked at the   ch-3 picot the center motif is attached.
- ⌘ Thread crochet or fine yarns works best for type of edging.

Tip # 270

⌘ This type of small motif, which is approximately 5 rounds, will extend a project 2- to 6- inches.

⌘ It can be used when a project needs to be enlarged without enlarging the center motif.

⌘ The Motif then has an edging to pull the entire item together as a unit.

TIP # 271
Intricate Designs Can Be Used As An Edging:

⌘ For example, a pineapple edging can take many rows to develop

⌘ This will add 4- to 6-inches to the garment, afghan, motif.

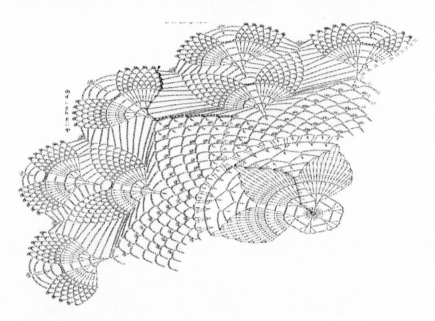

⌘   This type of edging becomes a focal point of placement.

Best Practices for this type of edging:

⌘   If the item crocheted is rather plain, or same stitch – crocheted in all dc, **this edging adds variety.**

⌘   If the edging is place on a crop-top sweater, **the waistline will become the focal point of the garment.**

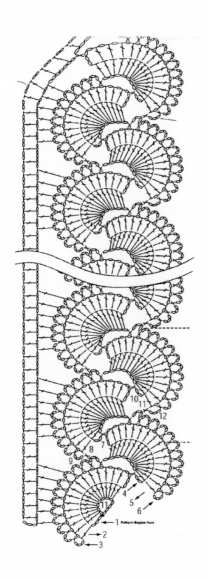

TIP # 272

Another Example of an Intricate Edging:
Some books refer to this type of edging as a Queen Anne's Lace

⌘   This type of edging is always worked as a separate piece, then attached to the afghan, garment or other item.

⌘   This type of edging can be used as a bookmark when worked in thread.

This pattern begins here at the bottom.
←←

TIP # 273
Combination Lacet and Shell Pattern.

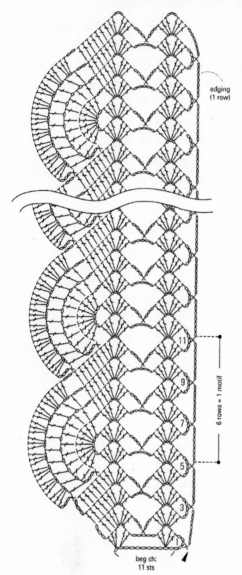

edging
(1 row)

11

9

7

5

3

6 rows = 1 motif

beg ch:
11 sts

⌘ The Bar & Lacet is primarily used in Filet Crochet.

⌘ Here the combination with a shell pattern worked as one piece is a versatile type of edging., which can also be used as a bookmark when worked in thread.

◄◄ This edging is worked from the bottom, then onto the side which forms the shell pattern.

TIPS # 274 - 282
Insertion Basics:

⌘ An insertion is a narrow piece of crochet, which is straight on both side edges.

⌘ Insertions can be "inserted" between two pieces of **crochet;**

⌘ Or an insertion can be inserted between two pieces of **fabric;**

⌘ Or an insertion can be crocheted between to purchased **trims.**

⌘ An insertion is usually from 2- to 12- inches in width at the widest portion.

⌘ Insertions can be created by working any stitch's pattern for an extended length.

⌘ Celtic Lace Crochet, Bruges Crochet, Bogen Band Crochet are forms of insertions. Entire projects can be created using these narrow strips of insertions. These forms of crochet are usually ½" to 1 ½" wide.

⌘ Filet Crochet can be used an insertion. In the 19TH & early 20TH Centuries, many "gentleladies" used insertions to border crinolines, dresses, and slip edgings.

⌘ An insertion can become the focal point in a project. For

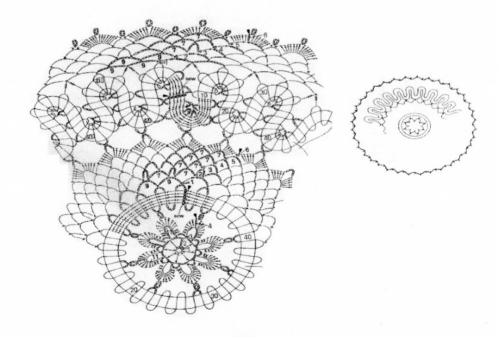

example: Celtic Lace pattern can be inserted in the doily.

TIP # 283

⌘ If a garment was made in "Granny" or other motifs, an insertion can be used to increase the garment's size, especially on children's garments since they grow extremely fast.

TIP # 284
EXAMPLES OF INSERTIONS

An insertion can be "inserted" between two pieces of crochet or two

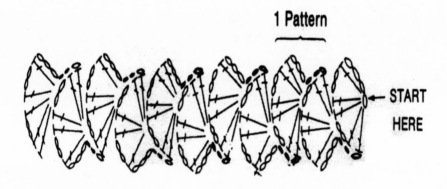

pieces of fabric.

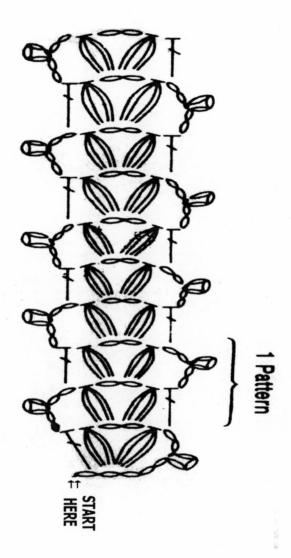

1 Pattern

↑↑
START
HERE

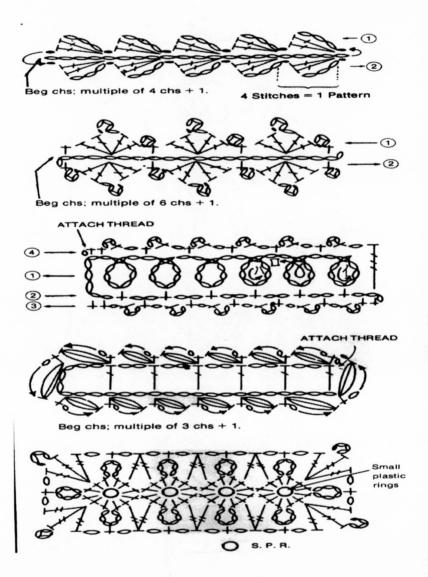

Beg chs; multiple of 4 chs + 1.

4 Stitches = 1 Pattern

Beg chs; multiple of 6 chs + 1.

ATTACH THREAD

ATTACH THREAD

Beg chs; multiple of 3 chs + 1.

Small
plastic
rings

◯ S. P. R.

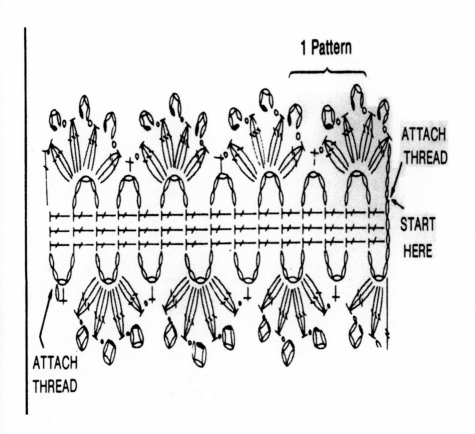

1 Pattern

ATTACH THREAD

START HERE

ATTACH THREAD

Basic Finishing Tips

Chapter 21

TIP # 285

The methods you use to finish your crochet depend mainly on what you are using the item for and what yarn or thread you have used.

TIP # 286

Crochet items always look better if you finish with some type of edging. The edging acts like a frame around the crochet item.

TIP # 287

Count all the stitches along border.   When approaching the corner, mark the first and last stitches with a safety pin or other marker.   This will be where corner stitches are placed on the several rows of the border pattern. Note that sometimes there are increase stitches in the corner in order to formulate the correct spacing for turn.

TIP # 288

Never begin to work an edging at the corner; start in the middle of the row.   Count all the stitches along the border and mark every 10th stitch.   It is easier to move markers than to rip and pull out hours of crochet work.

TIP # 289

There are several ways that you can join items together. Method 1: You can **use a needle and the same type yarn used to crochet the item** and whip stitch items together.   If you join in this manner, place the two fronts of motifs or garments together facing each other.   When ready to stitch, pick up the inside single loop of the top chain stitch. Do not pick up both parts of the chain as this will cause bulk between the joining and look very unprofessional.

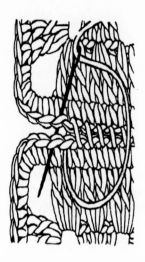 

TIP # 290

You can crochet items together with slip stitches; single crochet; half double crochet or double crochet.   To me, this method is better than whip stitching because the stitching remains evenly worked.

TIP # 291

The taller the stitch, the more space   that will naturally develop between the motifs or garments.   For example, double crochet stitches will create its own pattern between the stitches.

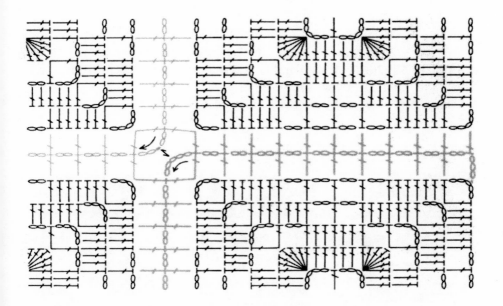

The above pattern is worked in symbol crochet stitches so you can have a schematic of the method.↑

1. Attach yarn to 2nd motif, ch 3. YO, insert hook into first motif's corner stitch
2. Insert hook as shown by arrow, into first motif and complete the double crochet. Ch 2. Skip 2 stitches. YO, insert hook into next stitch and pull thru.   See 3 loops on hook, YO and pull thru 2 loops, see 2 loops on hook. YO and insert hook into motif 1, YO and pull thru.   See 5 loops on hook. YO and pull thru all 5 loops.   (NOTE: the DC stitches between the motif will align with each other.   See symbol chart)   Follow symbol chart.

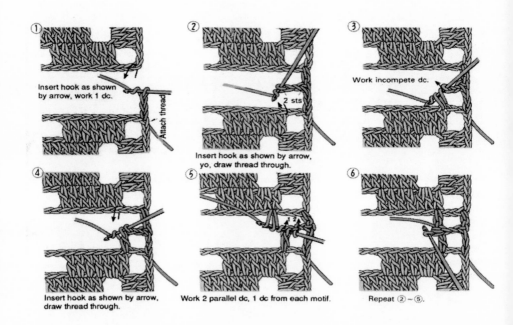

① Insert hook as shown by arrow, work 1 dc. Attach thread

② Insert hook as shown by arrow, yo, draw thread through. 2 sts

③ Work incompete dc.

④ Insert hook as shown by arrow, draw thread through.

⑤ Work 2 parallel dc, 1 dc from each motif.

⑥ Repeat ② ~ ⑤.

TIP # 292

I prefer to join with single crochet stitch rather than with slip stitch. Slip st needs a lot of elasticity, so therefore, you have to work the slip stitches very loosely. The slip stitch is a rigid and tight stitch with little stretch between the stitches. As in Method 1, place the two fronts of motifs or garment parts together facing each other. When ready to stitch, pick up the outside single loops of the top of single crochet stitch.

TIP #293

As you know, the top portion of a crochet stitch has two parts which appear to form a series of V's on their side (**>>>**). When joining, do not pick up both parts of the top of the stitch, as this will cause bulk between the joining and look very unprofessional. When the front of each piece is placed together facing one another, the pick up the front loop of the piece closest to you, and the back loop of the other piece.

For example, when joining, you have placed the two corresponding sides together, using markers to hold them in place, pick up the back loop from the back piece and the front loop from the front piece. This will form a neat join.

TIP # 294

You can use your Tunisian Crochet hook to join items together with a method that is called the **Tunisian Stitch Join.** You will need the yarn from the crochet items and size G (4.00mm) Tunisian hook (this is the crochet hook which is about 10" to 14" long—looks similar to a knitting needle with hook on the end. Also called a "Cro-hook", Afghan hook). With 2 motifs or garment pieces, place the two fronts facing together:
1. Pin the front sides of items facing each other to hold them in place while working
2. With joining yarn, make a slip knot and attach to the hook.
3. Insert the Tunisian hook into the front loop of the top chain on the item closest to you; and then insert the hook under the first back loop of the motif 2.

4. Yarn over, and pull through both loops. Yarn over and pull thru
    1 working loop. (see 2 loops on hook) Leave the working loops
    on the hook. NOTE: The working loops will accumulate on the
    Tunisian hook.

5. *Insert hook in next front stitch of Motif 1, and in the next back
    loop of motif 2, Yarn over, and pull through both loops. Yarn
    over pull thru 1 working loop to lock the two motif loops
    together, and leave working loop on hook*. Repeat from * to *
    across row until all working loops are on the Tunisian.   For
    example, if you have join 18 stitches from motifs 1 and 2, there
    should be 18 loops on the hook.

6. Working the loops off the hook in the following manner, is called the "Return" row: Yarn over and pull thru 1 loop, then *Yarn and pull thru 2 loops.* Repeat from * to * to end of row.   There will be 1 loop left on hook.

7. Cut working yarn with approximately 5" long. Finish off.
8. Weave in ends with smaller hook.

TIP # 295

Be very careful when "blocking" your crochet item.   Not all crochet items need to be "blocked".   Blocking is a term which is used when the finished crochet product is forced into a particular desired shape. You can force the crochet into the desired shape with heat, chemical, water, or natural gravity.

For example, you crochet a doily and it is not perfectly round, so you take the time to pin it into the round shape you desire and you can iron it into shape (Heat blocking);   you can starch it into shape (Chemical blocking; you can dampen the item with water in a spray bottle, then shape it (water blocking); or you can put a heavy book on the item and let gravity force it into shape. **(NOTE: sometimes, this can take a long time, and is not recommended if you are in a hurry).**

For example, you crochet a sweater, sometimes, depending upon the yarn or thread it is better to hang the garment on a padded hangar and let gravity shape the garment.

TIP # 296

When you take a crochet garment or item to the dry cleaners you have to give them specific instructions on how to clean a handmade garment. Not all dry cleaners are experienced in handling "Heirloom" quality cleaning.   This is the buzz word **"Heirloom Quality Cleaning."** The dry cleaners will take your garment through a manual process of cleaning instead of just throwing it in with all the other garments in vat. However, you have to tell them the following and have it written on your receipt, so you KNOW what you said.
   ♥ Heirloom quality cleaning
   ♥ Hand steamed
   ♥ **Do not Block** (Blocking to a dry cleaners mean to put the heavy pressing irons on your work flush it with high heat—this kills most crochet, and if there were textured stitches, they will be flatter than a pancake)
   ♥ **Fold, do not hang. (Everything in a cleaners is placed on wire hangars, which pull shoulders of garments out of shape.**

TIP #297

Every good label will give laundering instructions, please follow the laundering instructions given on the label.   See Chapter 14 with all the laundering symbols. When you give someone a gift of crochet item, include the label or a copy of the label's laundering instructions. They will know how to care for the handmade item.

Basic Crochet Garment Tips

Chapter 22

TIP # 298

When working from designer's pattern, take time to study the entire pattern layout.   There are several things a good pattern contains:

- ✓ Photo of the completed item
- ✓ Schematic of the pattern.   This is a graphic drawing of the pattern.   Measurements and dimensions may be placed on the graphic so that you can "see" what you are going to make.
- ✓ Featured stitch pattern.
- ✓ Optional: Featured stitch pattern in International crochet symbols.   Crochet symbols give you a "graphic" or schematic of the stitch pattern.
- ✓ Gauge dimensions.   Gauge is important when you are following a designer's pattern.   Gauge has two important measurements, which are created by a certain hook size with specific yarn: **The *horizontal gauge* is the number of *stitches* within a certain number of inches.**   For example, 12 dc stitches in 3 inches.   This means that the designer is getting 12 stitches on G (4.00mm or 4.25mm—see Chapter 9 for the difference) hook in "FruFru" yarn.   So when you make a sample swatch you should be getting 12 dc stitches in 3 inches on G (4.00 or 4.25mm) in "FruFru" yarn. **The *vertical* gauge is the number of *rows* within a certain number of inches.**   For example, the designer get 5 rows in 3 inches with the G hook and "FruFru" yarn.   You will need to get 5 rows in 3 inches.   If you are not matching the designer's dimensions exactly, then *YOU* have to make change.   The most important dimension of gauge is the *stitch gauge*.   If you are getting more stitches to the inches, for example 15 stitches in 3 inches, then you have to change your hook to a size larger.   If you are getting fewer stitches to the inches, then you have to change to smaller hook, for example you are getting 9 stitches, then you have to switch to F (3.75mm) hook.   *This is what is meant by "Take time to check your gauge", which appears in a lot of patterns.*
- ✓ Yarn type and information
- ✓ Tools, supplies, and notions
- ✓ If the pattern has unusual stitches or there is something that you need to know there should be a special notes section.

- ✓ Garment finished sizes
- ✓ Step-by-Step pattern instructions.

TIP # 299

If you don't like the yarn in the pattern or can't find the yarn in the pattern, you can make a **substitution in the type of yarn**. First, You have to make a gauge swatch with the new yarn at least 5 inches wide and 5 inches high (5" x 5"). Count the number of stitches in the center 3 inches; and count the number of rows in the center 3 inches. *__KNOW YOUR STITCH AND ROW COUNTS__ !*

TIP # 300

Compare your stitch and row counts to the gauge given in the pattern. Find the yarn information in the pattern to see how many yards the garment requires; compare the yarn you want to work with to the yarn in the pattern. For example, how many skeins or yards are called for in the pattern?? Check your yarn label to see how many yards are in the skein.

TIP # 301

Here's the Math worked out for you: Divide the total yards from the pattern by yards specified on the label of the replacement yarn. The result is the number of skeins or balls of yarn to purchase. For

example, 1,800 yds *(amount needed to make the sweater)* ÷ *by 251 yds on the ball you want to use = 7.18 skeins. So you have to buy 8 skeins to be sure you have enough yarn*.

TIP # 302

Don't purchase a substitute yarn by weight if pattern's yarn information is listed by "yards" and vis-à-vis. Not all same weights of yarns have the same yardage. Try to use yarns that have the same amount yards on the label.

Tip # 303

If the yarn you want to use is only listed by the weight on the label, you will need to do a little work. Buy a sample skein. With a permanent marker mark every yard for about 10 yards. (Mark more yards if you want to be more accurate). Crochet the yards in pattern stitch. Measure the swatches dimensions. For example: 10 yards of yarn measures 5" by 5" square. Multiply the length by the width to determine the square inches of crocheted fabric. This is 25 square inches. Weight the swatch. **You have to convert the weight of the yarn to yards of yarn.**

Tip # 304

To determine the number of **square inches of crocheted fabric** in a particular pattern stitch: swatch length   multiplied by (X) swatch width   = square inches of crochet fabric. This can be rectangle or square.

Tip # 305

Math for yarn required per square inch of fabric: Length of yarn $\div$ square inches of fabric = yarn per sq. in.   Referring to the schematic for the garment you want to make, figure out the square inches of fabric you need.   Be sure you total the square inches for all the various sweater parts.   If they are not "square" or rectangle, pretend they are, then do the math for that particular shape using Tip 304.

Tip # 306

✓ Make a photo copy of the garment pattern you want to make.
✓ Sometimes, you have to make changes to the pattern, or notes to the pattern. I have some "Post-It" notes which I write on, if I am working from a designer's pattern.
✓ Use color pencils or highlighters to indicate where all the *'s, ( )'s, [ ]'s and other repeats. I use a color pencil or highlighter for each type of pattern repeat.
✓ Keep the pattern, yarn label and the swatch in sheet protectors.

TIP # 307

Take a good set of body measurements.   No one ever matches up perfectly to the beautiful models in the pictures.   Detailed measurement charts are located in Chapter 24.   There are two set of measurements that go into the making of a crochet garment: Actual body measurements, and "ease" measurements.   You have to take your body measurements, no matter how large you are.   I have to give kudos to men; they know their measurements.

TIP # 308

Take a good set of measurements at least 3 times per year.   You may weigh more in the Winter months, because the body stores extra fat to keep warm or you may be more sedentary.   In the Spring and Summer months, you may see a change in the body shaping even though you weight the same;   fat may be converting to muscle mass.   Muscles weight more than fat. In the Autumn, most of us are more active, so the body changes again.

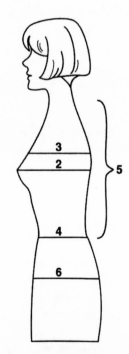

Chart from Simplicity Pattern Co. Inc

How To Measure:

✓ You may have to get someone to help you take accurate measurements if you can't measure yourself.

✓ Measure over the undergarments you normally wear.   Hold the tape measure comfortably snug, but not tight.

✓ HEIGHT: Standing against a flat wall without shoes, measure from floor to top of your head.

✓ BUST: (2 on chart) Around the fullest part of the bust and straight across the back.

✓ HIGH BUST OR CHEST: (3 on chart) Directly under the underarms, straight across the back and above the bust.

✓ WAIST: (4 on chart) Tie a piece of yarn around waist and let it settle naturally at your waistline, measure

over the yarn.   Keep the yarn in place for the next measurement.
- ✓ BACK WAIST LENGTH: (5 on chart). From the most prominent bone at the base of neck to the natural waistline.
- ✓ HIP: (6 on chart) Around body at fullest part, usually 7" to 9" below waist.

TIP # 309

Purchase a good "quilter's measuring tape.   These usually are 120" or more.

TIP # 310

There is a difference between the body's measurements and the Garment's measurements.   The difference between the two is called **_wearing ease"._** Wearing ease is vital.   This is the amount of extra inches that you have to add in order for the garment to fit well. The body must have wearing ease in order to function within the garment. When you work from commercial crochet patterns, the "ease factor" has been taken care of for you.

- ➤ Ease for the bust area: If you add a minimum of 4 inches to the fullest bust measurement, there is only 1 inch of ease on each side of the front pattern piece, and 1 inch on each side of the back pattern piece.
- ➤ Ease for the hips: Add a minimum of about 3 inches to the total hip measurement.   This is ¾" to each side, as you did for the bust. Add more ease if you have large hips.

TIP # 311

As you are working on the garment, review your progress often.   Stop a moment and try the garment on, even if you are only on row 3.   This is very important because if the garment is too small you will know right away rather than crocheting the entire garment and then finding out it is too small, too big, or doesn't fit at all.

TIP # 312

When crocheting garments in larger sizes, it is always better to err on the side of too much ease rather than too little.   Too little ease, makes the garment too tight and perhaps too uncomfortable. Too much ease gives the appearance of a "roomy" or oversized garment.

TIP # 313

When working on a garment's parts work on both similar parts at the same time.   For example, if you working on a pullover, work on the back and the front in the same sitting.   In this way your gauge will be the same on both parts in designated section.   If you are working on the sleeves, then work on both sleeves at the same time.

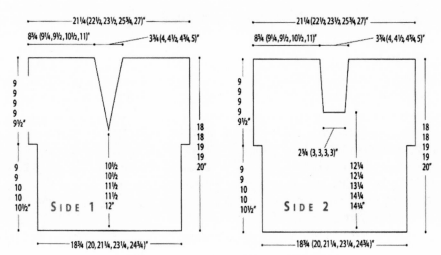

Graphic from CGOA: TODAY'S CROCHET

TIP # 314

The garment is usually supported by the neck and shoulders, and it drapes from there. Too much crochet fabric in a heavy yarn may be too much for the neck and shoulders to support. Use a yarn or thread that is light enough with a firm enough tensile strength to support the garment.

TIP # 315

When working on garments, never make your increases on the very beginning of the row or the very last stitch of the row. After you have crocheted 3 stitches, then make your increases for the garment.   The garment will hang better.

TIP # 316

When making sleeves, there are 4 key measurements: Wrist, Upper Arm, Underarm sleeve length, and the armhole depth.   You have to add a minimum of 2 inches of ease to the wrist measurement; or measure the circumference of the fist. Add 2" of ease to the upper arm measurement.

TIP # 317

QUESTION: *WHAT DO I WANT TO ACCOMPLISH WITH THIS PROJECT ??!!??* Each time you start a new project you have to ask yourself that question.   In other words, I recommend you interview yourself or the receiver of the project before you spend a lot of time and effort crocheting.   You may "think" you know what the person may like, especially if it is a gift, then be sorely insulted because you didn't interview them.

- ♥ How is garment going to used?? Casual or business, or evening. Types of yarns selected will determine this answer.
- ♥ What is the fashion value? Will it be a fad, which most young people and teens like; or will it be a classic, which most adults like. (Adults want a garment they may be able to wear over several seasons or even over several years—and it still looks great)
- ♥ Is the garment for warm or cool weather?? Again pay close attention to the type of yarn selected for the project.
- ♥ Does the person have allergies or sensitivity to a particular type of yarn.   For example,   is the person allergic to wool; is cotton to stiff for their skin.
- ♥ How is the project to be laundered or cleaned? Check the yarn label
- ♥ What other items in a person's wardrobe will complement the garment you will be making.
- ♥ What is the person's figure type?
  - o Inverted Triangle—heavy on upper portion of the body

- o Rectangle—same measurements for bust, waist, and hips.
- o Hourglass—same measurement for bust and hips, but very small waistline.
- o Short/Petite
- o Large or slim upper arms
- o Round shoulders.

TIP # 318

When working on a garment from a crochet pattern book, compare the measurements from the schematic to the measurements of one of your favorite sweaters, then chose the size of the measurements, which closely align with the garment's measurements that fit you.

TIP # 319

How much yarn to buy is always an issue.   Most crocheters are in the habit of purchasing too much yarn for your projects—hence we end up with a stash of odd lots of yarn.   The following two charts provide an estimate for how much yarn to purchase for garment projects, especially when you are not using the yarn recommended in the pattern.   See chart on next page.

FIT FLATTER THE QUEEN (SIZED)
ADULT SIZING CHARTS

MEASUREMENTS	SIZE A	SIZE B	SIZE C	SIZE D	SIZE E	SIZE F
Actual Bust Measurements in inches	32-34	36-38	40-42	44-46	48-50	52-54
Finished Bust Measurements in inches	40	44	48	51	55	59
Actual Bust Measurements in cm	81-86	91-97	102-107	112-117	122-127	132-137
Finished Bust Measurements in cm	102	112	122	130	140	150

NOTES: 1. THE NUMBERS BELOW ARE AN APPROXIMATION AND ARE NOT TO BE TAKEN AS EXACT YARDAGE. 2. MORE YARDAGE WILL BE NEED FOR DIFFICULT STITCH PATTERNS SUCH AS POST STITCHES OR POPOCORNS 3. IF YOU ARE MAKING A GARMENT WITH POCKETS, YOU WILL NEED 2 EXTRA SKEINS OF YARN.

Amount needed for Class 2 Yarns: Sport or DK weight with Approx 330 yards to the skein & approx 6 stitches to inch gauge	Yards per skein	SIZE A	SIZE B	SIZE C	SIZE D	SIZE E	SIZE F
Tank top, vest, or camisole top	330	1068.00	1137.50	1248.00	1430.00	1690.00	1950.00
Short Sleeve	330	1235.00	1365.00	1495.00	1755.00	1950.00	2145.00
V Neck Pullover/Cardigan Long Sleeved	330	1690.00	1820.00	2080.00	2340.00	2600.00	2860.00
Crew Neck Pullover/Cardigan Long Sleeved	330	1859.00	2002.00	2288.00	2574.00	2860.00	3146.00
Turtle Neck Pullover/Cardigan Long Sleeved	330	2044.90	2202.20	2516.80	2831.40	3146.00	3460.60

Amount needed for Class 3 Yarn: Worsted Wgt; Approx 210 yds/skein. Approx Gauge: 4 1/2 to 5 stitches per inch	Yards per skein	SIZE A	SIZE B	SIZE C	SIZE D	SIZE E	SIZE F
Vest	210	910	975	1072.5	1235	1430	1625
Short Sleeve	210	1040.00	1170.00	1300.00	1500.00	1690.00	1885.00
V Neck Pullover/Cardigan Long Sleeved	210	1365	1500	1625	1755	2210	2535
Crew Neck Pullover/Cardigan Long Sleeved	210	1501.50	1650.00	1787.50	1930.50	2431.00	2788.50
Turtle Neck Pullover/Cardigan Long Sleeved	210	1651.65	1815.00	1996.25	2123.55	2674.10	3067.35

FIT FLATTER THE QUEEN (SIZED)
ADULT SIZING CHARTS

Amount need for Class 4 Yarn: Bulky Wgt; Approx 150 yds/skein. Approx Gauge: 3 to 4 stitches per inch	Yards per skein	SIZE A	SIZE B	SIZE C	SIZE D	SIZE E	SIZE F
Vest	150	780	845	910	1040	1170	1300
Short Sleeve	150	975	1040	1137.5	1300	1462.5	1657.5
V Neck Pullover/Cardigan Long Sleeved	150	1170	1300	1430	1560	1560	2080
Crew Neck Pullover/Cardigan Long Sleeved	150	1287.00	1430.00	1573.00	1716.00	1716.00	2288.00
Turtle Neck Pullover/Cardigan Long Sleeved	150	1415.70	1573.00	1730.30	1887.60	1887.60	2516.80

NOTES FOR ME

LAST UPDATED: 1/4/2009

2 of 2

336 Crochet Tips !
The Solutions Book For Crocheters

Tɪᴘ # 320

Take time to enjoy the creative process when you are working on your garment pattern. The designer had fun and enjoyed the creative process; and if you are following muse, you can enjoy the creative process as well. The creative process is not just some "anything goes" process it is a disciplined process. Here are the ABC's of the creative process for garments:

- ❖ A   =   Always measure.
  - ▪ Measure, your body, your garment, your schematic.
- ❖ B   =   Begin with a Gauge swatch
- ❖ C   =   Choose your stitches & equipment
  - ▪ Choosing the correct yarn is vital.
- ❖ D   =   Develop the designer's pattern into a pattern that fits you. Use her pattern for your personal use—this is why patterns are sold.
  - ▪ To develop a designer's pattern for your publication use, without giving credit or asking permission to use the pattern, is an invasion of the U. S. Copyright Law; and the designer has the right to sue you.
- ❖ E   =   Et Cetera and everything else that helps your garment to fit. Use *336 Crochet Tips!* to help you through the process.

Tɪᴘ # 321

Keep and Maintain a Project log of your crochet project. When you have to amend the pattern to make it fit you, it is vital that you maintain a project log. Because the crochet project is a work in progress, you may not remember or recall "how" you did a particular step. If you can refer back to your notes, you can "pick up where you left off". (NOTE: if you would like to purchase a project log syllabus, contact Designs 4 Crochet LLc, P O Box 6904, West Palm Beach, FL 33405; Cost is $7.95 plus $2.00 shipping and handling.

MY GARMENT TIPS AND NOTES:

Crochet Inspiration

Idea Tips

Chapter 23

TIP # 322

Ideas for crochet are everywhere.   Just open your intuitive spirit. Become aware of your surroundings.

TIP # 323

The key question to ask yourself when searching for new ideas for your crochet projects is: *What if ??*   Once you ask yourself "What if??" pay attention to your intuition. If you allow, your intuition to become activated, it will "speak" to you as a "still small voice". Ideas and answers will begin to come to you in response to *"What if ??*

TIP # 324

For ideas about colorways and color patterns, pick out a beautiful State Park or Public Garden.   Pay attention to how nature colors, and take some written notes when you go visit those gardens and parks.

TIP # 325

If you can't go to nature to see how nature colors, then purchase a color wheel. The Johannes Itten Color Star is an excellent tool , which will allow you to see how colors juxtapose. Rainbow Color Selector by Knit 1 Crochet 2 is another excellent color wheel. You can also try the "Quilter's Color Wheel" or the "Artist's Color Wheel". These color wheels have placed all colors in a perspective that allows you to select contrast colors; triad colors, primary colors, colors that blend; warm colors also known as aggressive colors; cool color also known as receding colors; complementary colors; analogous colors, monochromatic colors of the same value; counterpoint colors; and finally multi-color combinations.. A color wheel of your choice is a must in your crochet kit when you are selecting colors for a project.

TIP # 326

Take a trip through your favorite department stores.
Whoa !! "not to Shop til' you drop"; however, to just look at the color patterns of clothes, linens, home décor in the store. You see, stores have to take color instructions from Pantone Color Institute. They have to know what colors will be in vogue 6 months from now, a year or two

from now.   So, if you want to know what colors will be in style in six months visit your local department store just to pay attention to the color patterns throughout the store. The Color Institute sets what colors cars will be; what colors will be in style for home décor, furniture and other items; what paints will be available at your local home repair or paint store.   All stores follow market color trends. Here is a short list of stores which follow Market trends and follow by the Pantone or The Color Institute: Stein Mart stores; Costco Warehouse; Target Stores; Home Goods; Michael's; JoAnn's; A. C. Moore stores; Hobby Lobby; Marshall's; Macy's; Palm Beach Gardens Mall; Wellington Mall, or your local mall; Walgreens Pharmacy; Rooms-to-Go Furniture Stores; Wal-Mart stores; plus many other stores and businesses. So stroll through your local store, not only to shop, however, to pay attention to colors. Crochet your projects in vogue colors.

TIP # 327

The healthy human eye, which does not have the color blind trait (usually found in men), can distinguish more than 2000 distinct colors. Color really does matter.   Studies show that some colors cause various people to react various ways, both pleasant and unpleasant to the dominant colors around them.   Some people glow and are most happy with any shade of "red".   This same color will have a negative effect on other people.   Simply ask a person whether they like or dislike a particular color if you are making a project for them.   If you like red, but the person you are making a gift for hates red, they will never wear your special project and your crochet efforts will be for naught. *COLOR MATTERS !! USE IT TO YOUR ADVANTAGE.*

TIP # 328

Ideas for crochet projects can come from observing the architecture of great buildings. Take a hometown trip just to view the great buildings in your area. Be sure to take your notebook and sketch pencils with you.   If you like to crochet geometric patterns, look at building trimmings; iif you like to crochet texture, look at the buildings and their windows.

TIP # 329

If you only crochet, then look at knit books and visit knit stores. Knitters have a whole other view of the fiber arts world, so step in to it. I know, some local yarn stores (LYS) don't want crocheters in their stores, but none-the-less, VISIT ANYHOW.   Here is hoping that you will support your LYS.   However, visit to look at colors; visit to get ideas; visit to get a new perspective; visit to be defiant by purchasing a skein and just sitting there to crochet.

TIP # 330

Ideas come from looking at commercial graphic logos.   Look at the "Coca Cola logo"; The IBM logo; Delta Air Lines logo.   Look at the graphic logos of major companies. If you love to make motifs, these will provide lots of inspiration.

TIP # 331

Remember to
C-R-O-C-H-E-T
Each Day:

C	*Challenge* **yourself with your personal best**
R	*Review; Refine; Relax;* **and** *Remain* **Intuitively Aware.**
O	*Organize* **for Action;** *Optimism* **Invites** *Opportunities* **for positive synergy.**
C	*Create* **something memorable;** *Create* **Prosperity**
H	*Have* **Fun;** *Have* **Serendipity;** *Have* **Synergy**
E	*Explore* **your possibilities with** *Excitement.*
T	*Transform* **your passion, positively.**

TIP # 332

Ideas for your crochet projects are everywhere—Look up—sometimes the clouds form interesting patterns, look down—sometimes nature forms interesting patterns; pay attention to buildings and their trims and borders—perhaps some ideas will come through;   look within—"What if??"; and definitely pay attention to the yarn—I swear, it speaks to me intuitively; and it will intuitively speak to you, as well.

Ask children. They have a wealth of ideas. The local Costco Warehouse or office supply store sells a collection of 84 color pens in a set.   Ask a child to pick colors for you from this set; and you will be amazed at the color combinations children select. They have innocent instinct—use it. Ask children what they think about your crochet ideas--they have wonderful ideas;   simply listen to them.   The children will be so proud if you can show them how you used their idea for your crochet project.

INSPIRATION NOTES:

INSPIRATION NOTES:

INSPIRATION NOTES:

Crochet Sources and
Resources Tips

Chapter 24

336 Crochet Tips !
The Solutions Book for Crocheters

336 Crochet Tips !
The Solutions Book for Crocheters

TIP # 333

No one travels any journey alone.   Many people have helped me to this point.   Family, friends, students who took the chance to take my classes and sit with me while I entertained what seemed like "far-fetched What if" crochet ideas; Crochet Professionals who embraced my ideas and encouraged me to move forward; a few Crochet Professionals who rejected my ideas and hoped that I would vanish and give up—but I didn't. (Those are the ones who made me strong enough to just keep going).

"Be ever so grateful, and be ye ever so humble", as my great-grand-mother use to say. I am grateful to you; and thankful for you. You helped me to this point, and I hope I have helped you. We give thanks.

Who has helped you with your crochet project ??

Express gratitude !

Tɪᴘ # 334
There is always someone who cares enough to support you

**(Cᴏʀᴘᴏʀᴀᴛɪᴏɴs ᴡʜᴏ sᴜᴘᴘᴏʀᴛᴇᴅ ᴍᴇ
ᴀʟᴏɴɢ ᴛʜᴇ ᴡᴀʏ)**

Rᴇsᴏᴜʀᴄᴇs

1. **Great Balls of Yarn** (my local yarn store)
   319 Belvedere Road
   West Palm Beach, Florida.
   Phone: 561-651-1225
   Fax: 561-659-0144
   Email: info@greatballsofyarn.com

2. **Just Imaginknit** (my local yarn store)
   6663 B Lake Worth Road, Lake Worth, Florida 33467
   Phone: 561.433.3444
   Fax: 561.433.5133
   Email: Info@JustImaginKnit.net

3. Coats & Clark, Greenville, SC, www.coats.com

4. Berroco Yarn Company, Uxbridge, MA, www.berroco.com

5. Caron Yarn Company, Washington, NC, www.caron.com; and
   www.naturallycaron.com

6. Patons Yarns, Ontario, Canada,
   www.patonyarns.com

7. Boye; Wrights Incorporated, Antioch, TN 37013
   1-888-39HELP6
   (1-888-394-3576)
   help@wrights.com

TIP # 335
BIBLIOGRAPHY

1. <u>Crochet Tips !</u> (The Original editions) by Joan A. Davis, copyright 1993-2008
2. <u>Crochet to Fit and Flatter the Queen-Sized</u> by Joan A. Davis, Certified Crochet Instruct, copyright 1993-2007.
3. <u>Merry Go Round the Pi (3.14159): The Basics of Creating Rounds</u> by Joan A. Davis, Copyright 2007
4. <u>Pineapples Pizzazz: The basics of Creating Pineapple Patterns</u>, Copyright 2007 by Joan A. Davis.
5. <u>Celtic Lace Crochet I & II,</u> copyright 2006 – 2008 by Joan A. Davis
6. <u>Magical Trapezoid Wrap</u>, copyright 2006 by Joan A. Davis
7. <u>Simplicity Teaching Kit Pattern Collection, Spring/Summer 2009</u> copyright 2009 by The Simplicity Pattern Co. Inc. www.simplicity.com
8. <u>Patons Back to Basics II</u> copyright by Coats Patons-Coats Canada Inc, 1992. www.patonyarns.com
9. <u>Crocheted Sweaters: Simple Stitches, Great Designs</u> copyright 2001 by Susan Huxley, Published by Martingale & Co.
10. <u>Today's Crochet: Sweaters from the Crochet Guild of America</u>, copyright 2003 by Susan Huxley, Published by Martingale & Co.
11. <u>America's Crochet Book,</u> copyright 1972 by Gertrude Taylor. Published Charles Scribner's Sons.
12. <u>Crochet Your Way</u>. Copyright 2000 by Gloria Tracy and Susan Levin. Published by The Taunton Books & Videos Press, Inc.
13. <u>Crochet in Plain English</u>. Copyright by Maggie Righetti. Published by St. Martin's Press.
14. <u>Sweater Design in Plain English</u>. Copyright 1990 by Maggie Righetti. Published by St. Martin's Press.
15. <u>Stitches, Patterns and Projects for Crocheting</u>. Copyright 1978 and 1983 in Italian. Translated by Sylvia Mulcahy. Published by Harper Colophon Books.

336 Crochet Tips !
The Solutions Book for Crocheters

16. I Taught Myself To Crochet. Copyright 1987 by The Boye Needle Company.
17. Improve Your Crochet Finishing.   Written by Barbara Johnson. Copyright 1978 by Leisure Arts.
18. Ondori Publication ISBN: 4-277-15512-Xc507 Japanese Book of Crochet Techniques. Copyright 1971
19. Nihon Vogue Book of Crochet Designs 200 Stitches, NV7193. ISBN 4-529-02198X C5077 P1900E (Japanese Publication).
20. Nihon Vogue Book of Motifs & Edgings 200 Patterns NV 7174.   ISBN 4-529-02072x-C5077 P1600E. (Japanese Publication).
21. Magic Crochet Magazines
22. Decorative Crochet Magazines
23. Self Publishing for Fiber Artists. Copyright 2008 by Myra Wood.

Body Measurements

Babies' - For infants who are not yet walking.

Sizes	XXS	XS	Small	Medium	Large
Weight	up to 7 lbs.	7-13 lbs.	13-18 lbs.	18-21 lbs.	21-24 lbs.
Approx. Height	up to 17"	17"-24"	24"-26½"	26½-31"	31"-34"

Toddlers' - For figures that are taller than Babies but shorter than Children. Pants have a diaper allowance; dresses are shorter than Children's sizes.

Sizes	½	1	2	3	4	
Chest	19	20	21	22	23	In
Waist	19	19½	20	20½	21	"
Approx. Height	28	31	34	37	40	"

Child's

Sizes	2	3	4	5	6	6X	7	8	
Chest	21	22	23	24	25	25½	26	27	In
Waist	20	20½	21	21½	22	22½	23	23½	"
Hip	—	—	24	25	26	26½	27	28	"
Back Waist Length	8½	9	9½	10	10½	10¾	11½	12	"
Approx. Height	35	38	41	44	47	48	50	52	"

Girls'/Girls' Plus - For the growing girl who has not yet begun to mature.
Girls' Plus are designed for girl's over the average weight for their age and height.

Sizes	Girls						Girls' Plus					
	7	8	10	12	14	16	8½	10½	12½	14½	16½	
Chest	26	27	28½	30	32	34	30	31½	33	34½	36	In
Waist	23	23½	24½	25½	26½	27½	28	29	30	31	32	"
Hip	27	28	30	32	34	36	33	34½	36	37½	39	"
Back Waist Length	11½	12	12¾	13½	14¼	15	12½	13¼	14	14¾	15½	"
Approx. Height	50	52	56	58½	61	61½	52	56	58½	61	63½	"

Junior

Sizes	3/4	5/6	7/8	9/10	11/12	13/14	15/16	17/18	19/20	21/22	23/24	
Bust	28	29	30½	32	33½	35	36½	38½	40½	42½	44½	In
Waist	22	23	24	25	26	27	28	29½	31	33½	35½	"
Hip-7" below waist	31	32	33½	35	36½	38	39½	41½	43½	45½	47½	"
Back Waist Length	13½	14	14½	15	15⅜	15¾	16⅛	16⅜	16⅝	16⅞	17⅛	"

Junior Plus

Sizes	13/14+	15/16+	17/18+	19/20+	21/22+	23/24+	25/26+	27/28+	29/30+	31/32+	
Bust	39½	41	42½	44	45½	47½	49½	51½	53½	55½	In
Waist	32½	33½	34½	35½	37	38½	40	41½	43	44½	"
Hip-7" below waist	41½	43	44½	46	47½	49½	51½	53½	55½	57½	"
Back Waist Length	15¾	16	16¼	16½	16¾	17	17¼	17½	17¾	18	"

Misses'/Miss Petite - For well-proportioned, developed figures.
Misses' about 5' 5" to 5' 6" without shoes. Miss Petite under 5' 4" without shoes.

Sizes	4	6	8	10	12	14	16	18	20	22	24	26	
Sizes-European	30	32	34	36	38	40	42	44	46	48	50	52	
Bust	29½	30½	31½	32½	34	36	38	40	42	44	46	48	In
Waist	22	23	24	25	26½	28	30	32	34	37	39	41½	"
Hip-9" below waist	31½	32½	33½	34½	36	38	40	42	44	46	48	50	"
Back Waist Length	15¼	15½	15¾	16	16¼	16½	16¾	17	17¼	17⅜	17½	17⅝	"
Petite-Back Waist Length	14¼	14½	14¾	15	15¼	15½	15¾	16	16¼	16⅜	16½	16⅝	"

Women's/Women's Petite - For the larger, more fully mature figures.
Women's about 5' 5" to 5' 6" without shoes. Women's Petite under 5' 4" without shoes.

Sizes	18W	20W	22W	24W	26W	28W	30W	32W	
Sizes-European	44	46	48	50	52	54	56	58	
Bust	40	42	44	46	48	50	52	54	In
Waist	33	35	37	39	41½	44	46½	49	"
Hip-9" below waist	42	44	46	48	50	52	54	56	"
Back Waist Length	17⅛	17¼	17⅜	17½	17⅝	17¾	17⅞	18	"
Petite-Back Waist Length	16⅛	16¼	16⅜	16½	16⅝	16¾	16⅞	17	"

Unisex - For figures within Misses', Men's, Teen-Boys, Boys' and Girl's size ranges.

Sizes	XXS	XS	S	M	L	XL	XXL	
Chest/Bust	28-29	30-32	34-36	38-40	42-44	46-48	50-52	In
Hip	29-30	31-32½	35-37	39-41	43-45	47-49	51-53	"

Boys' & Teen Boys' - For growing boys and young men who have not reached full adult stature.

Sizes	7	8	10	12	14	16	18	20	
Chest	26	27	28	30	32	33½	35	36½	In
Waist	23	24	25	26	27	28	29	30	"
Hip	27	28	29½	31	32½	34¼	35½	37	"
Neck Band	11¾	12	12½	13	13½	14	14½	15	"
Approx. Height	48	50	54	58	61	64	66	68	"
Shirt Sleeve	22¾	23¾	25	26¾	29	30	31	32	"

Men's - For men of average build; about 5' 10" without shoes.

Sizes	32	34	36	38	40	42	44	46	48	50	52	
Sizes-Eur/Fr	42	44	46	48	50	52	54	56	58	60	62	
Chest	32	34	36	38	40	42	44	46	48	50	52	In
Waist	27	28	30	32	34	36	39	42	44	46	48	"
Hip	34	35	37	39	41	43	45	47	49	51	53	"
Neck Band	13½	14	14½	15	15½	16	16½	17	17½	18	18½	"
Shirt Sleeve	31	32	32	33	33	34	34	35	35	36	36	"

Chart from Simplicity Pattern Co. Inc

TIP # 336

You have only just begun. Just acknowledge your surroundings, and keep crocheting—we will love you forever. By purchasing the patterns, the books, the yarns, the tools, visiting the websites; blogging to crocheters; connecting; networking; giving, sharing; receiving, you are supporting a network that binds the crochet world together with Intuitive Love, Agape Love, Universal Love, Sisterly Love. And according to an Ancient Book of Wisdom "...and the Greatest of these is Love...I Corinthians 13". May the Angels of Intuition, of Crochet, of Creativity, and The Angels of Love surround you; May all your crochet projects be a success!

ACKNOWLEDGEMENTS

To God be the Glory; To the Angels who "Kept Watch". In an ancient *Holy Bible*, there is a parable about 10 lepers who were placed in a camp for diseased people. 10 of the people were healed, and moved on with their lives. One returned to the Healer, to say thank you. The Healer asked, "Did I not heal 10 of you??" The one who returned, humbled himself, and said "Thank You" again. "No one is an island". It took many people helping me along the way, and I want to say thank you—I wish I could say thank you individually.

To family who kept asking when the book is going to be finished ?? To friends like Joyce Renee Wyatt, who just helped me to "get out there, and do your best"; To Myra Wood, who supported my classes by taking a class, bought my Tropical Maiden bejeweled bra at the Silent Auction, then gave me the road map to get this project completed; To Carol Bartlebaugh, who would just invite me over so loneliness would not sink in, traveled with me to many crochet conferences, and just for "being there", when "there" was all there was.

To the Faculty and Staff of Jeaga Middle School, West Palm Beach, FL, who kept me inspired, often when tears were in my eyes. To the crochet students all over Palm Beach County who would ask me every crochet-related question known—What they did not know that students in various locations were asking the same question. They loved crochet enough to take many classes from me. This is when I realized that *336 CROCHET TIPS !* was born. To the School District of Palm Beach County Adult & Community Education Program, which has allowed me to teach crochet since 2000.

To the Team at Lightning Source for helping the team at Designs 4 Crochet.

To my Special Friend, who kept me dancing to relieve stress; of course to my pet, Opportunity, who would look at me in awe, yawn, and keep on sleeping. There are more who helped, however the small space will not hold all the individual names, however, please know I Thank you.

ABOUT THE AUTHOR

Joan A. Davis is a certified crochet instructor with the Craft Yarn Council of America and Crochet Design of England, Part 1.   She has been crocheting professionally since 1987.   Founding member of the Crochet Guild of America and taught classes at the First CGOA Annual Conference in Chicago, IL at DePauw University.

In 2002, Joan was the Chairperson of The Tropical Crochet Guild of the Palm Beaches and spearheaded the Chapter's hosting of the national CGOA Conference in Palm Beach Gardens, Florida.   Joan has traveled extensively teaching crochet techniques for The Knit and Crochet Shows Produced by Offinger Manager, which produces the CGOA conferences.

Joan A. Davis teaches crochet classes for the Palm Beach County School District's Adult & Community Education Program since 2000.   More than 500 students have taken classes from her.

She is published in *Crochet Fantasy Magazines (All American Crafts Publications); Donna Kooler's Crochet Afghan Book; Fabulous Crocheted Ponchos* and *Crochet! Magazine.*

Joan lives in Riviera Beach, Florida with her pet cat, Opportunity.

ATTENTION TEACHERS:

DESIGNS 4 CROCHET LLC ENCOURAGES YOU TO USE THIS BOOK FOR TEACHING CROCHET. SUBJECT TO RESTRICTIONS STATED ON THE COPYRIGHT PAGE AND THE U. S. COPYRIGHT LAWS. USE THIS BOOK IN CONJUNCTION WITH ITS SYLLABUS FOR A COMPLETE CROCHET EDUCATION. HOWEVER, THE AUTHOR, JOAN A. DAVIS, RESPECTFULLY REQUEST THAT YOU ACKNOWLEDGE THE COPYRIGHT LAWS OF THE UNITED STATES OF AMERICA, AND HAVE STUDENTS PURCHASE THE BOOK RATHER THAN PHOTOCOPY THE BOOK

TEACHER DISCOUNT: 15 % OFF THE TEACHER'S COPY FOR EVERY QUANTITY OF 5 OR MORE BOOKS PURCHASED ON ONE ORDER TO ONE ADDRESS. DISCOUNT ON THE SYLLABUS FOR EVERY 5 OR MORE PURCHASED ON ONE ORDER TO ONE ADDRESS: $8.95 WITH 5% DISCOUNT.

QUANTITY DISCOUNTS APPLY, SEE THE ORDER FORM. TO CLAIM YOUR TEACHER DISCOUNT, PLEASE SIGN BELOW AND COMPLETE THE ORDER FORM ON THE BACK OF THIS PAGE.

ALLOW 3 WEEKS FOR DELIVERY OF BOOK(S) AND SYLLABUS.

336 Crochet Tips !
Order Form

I would like to order _____ copy(ies) of **336 Crochet Tips ! The Solutions Book for Crocheters.** $21.95 each (Florida Residents add 6.5% Sales Tax). Syllabus is $8.95 each. Quantity discount for more than 5 or more copies on one order—mailed to one address, receive a **5% discount.**   Check or money order in US Dollars drawn on a U. S. Bank.

Add Shipping and Handling: $4.50 for up to 3 books; 4 - 10 books, add $7.50 Shipping and Handling.   On quantities larger than 10 books, **Shipping and Handling is 10% of total order.**

Make Check or Money Order Payable to :   **Joan A. Davis, Author c/o Designs 4 Crochet LLC**

Name: _____

Address: _____

City: _____State _____ Zip_____

Email Address:

_____

If purchased from a bookseller, please list the Bookseller:

_____

City: _____ State: _____

Please advise how *336 Crochet Tips !* has helped you improve your crochet skills

Joan A. Davis
Designs 4 Crochet LLc
P O Box 6904
West Palm Beach, FL   33405
Email address: a0crochetjad@msn.com

336 Crochet Tips !
The Solutions Book for Crocheters

INDEX

Crochet Sources and Resources Tips   Chapter 24

336 Crochet Tips !
The Solutions Book for Crocheters

Crochet Sources and Resources Tips Chapter 24

A
DESIGNS 4 CROCHET LLC
PUBLICATION

MISSION STATEMENT
TEACHING THE LOVE OF CROCHET TO ONE PERSON AT A TIME

336 Crochet Tips !
The Solutions Book for Crocheters

Printed in the United States
221138BV00001B/1/P